Delivering Grace

As illustrated in the words and ways of the prophet Elisha

J T Mawson

Scripture Truth Publications

DELIVERING GRACE

First published 1932 by Pickering & Inglis, London (& Central Bible Truth Depot, London)

Reprinted c1946 by Central Bible Truth Depot, London

Reprinted with amended/additional references 2007 by Scripture Truth

Transferred to Digital Printing 2007

ISBN: 978-0-901860-64-4 (paperback)

ISBN: 978-0-901860-78-1 (hardback)

A publication of Scripture Truth

Scripture quotations, unless otherwise indicated, are taken from The Authorized (King James) Version. Rights in the Authorized Version are vested in the Crown. Reproduced by permission of the Crown's patentee, Cambridge University Press.

Cover photograph ©iStockphoto.com/Ynot2 (Gilad Levy)

Published by Scripture Truth Publications
Coopies Way, Coopies Lane,
Morpeth, Northumberland, NE61 6JN

Scripture Truth is an imprint of Central Bible Hammond Trust, a charitable trust

Typesetting by John Rice
Printed by Lightning Source

Foreword

Great words and wise were those that came last from the pen of Simon Peter for the flock of God that he loved so well. He was about to put off his tabernacle, for thus he described his coming martyrdom—what should he say to those who had still to face the many questions and difficulties that would arise in their personal experiences, and who had to go through the vicissitudes of life in the world of which Satan is the god? He had had an up and down experience himself. What had carried him through it and made him more than a conqueror at the end of it? Grace and the knowledge of our Lord and Saviour Jesus Christ. He could not separate the grace from the One in Whom it is, nor did he attempt it, so he wrote: "GROW IN GRACE, AND IN THE KNOWLEDGE OF OUR LORD AND SAVIOUR JESUS CHRIST. TO HIM BE GLORY, BOTH NOW AND FOR EVER. AMEN." He could add nothing to that. In that lay the secret of every spiritual deliverance and of all true victory and joy, and with that he closed his devoted life and service to the Lord and His flock. It is with the earnest hope that I may be able to help some at least of that blood-purchased flock to grow in grace and in the knowledge of our Lord and Saviour Jesus Christ, that I issue these Talks on Elisha, the prophet of grace.

J. T. Mawson

DELIVERING GRACE

Contents

"And Elisha Went Over"

HOW THE LORD REACHED
THE THRONE OF GRACE

"He took up also the mantle of Elijah, and went back and stood by the bank of Jordan. He took also the mantle of Elijah that fell from him, and smote the waters, and said, Where is the LORD God of Elijah? And when he had smitten the waters, they parted hither and thither, and Elisha went over. And when the sons of the prophets which were to view at Jericho saw him ... They came to meet him, and bowed themselves to the ground before him."

2 KINGS 2:13-15

Chapter 1
"And Elisha Went Over"

A crowd of young men, fifty or more, stand eagerly watching a lone figure as he descends the steep bank of the river. They sorely feel their need of a leader and head, and this man may be he. They are not sure, but the way that he crosses that turbulent flood will decide them. It is a momentous time, a time of crisis both for them and for him. His way with the river is very simple: he does but smite it with his mantle and call upon God, and lo, the waters part hither and thither, and he passes over as one would tread a beaten highway. And that crowd to a man bow down to the ground before him. They recognise his power and own him as their lord and head and leader.

The man that they acknowledged was Elisha, the God-appointed prophet to Israel. His name means "God is Saviour", and he represented a Saviour-God, Who was full of grace for a needy and stricken people. Of all the men who served God in those Old Testament days, he stands out as the prophet of grace, and in that he was a foreshadow of our Lord Jesus Christ in His present place on the Throne of Grace in Heaven, the Administrator of the grace of God to men. Only a shadow, mark you, and not the very image of Him, and as the shadow is nothing and the Substance is everything, so Elisha is nothing, except as his thrilling story does pictorially set before us the all-sufficient grace of our Lord Jesus Christ. And that is something, and well worthy of our study, for who can do without the Saviour and His grace? Not I, nor you, my reader and friend, whom I greet in this little book. The procession of needy folk with their burdens and ills and problems and sorrows pass before Elisha in its pages. We watch them as they come and go, and recognise our own spiritual needs portrayed in them; but as Elisha was the man for them all, so is his great Antitype the Man for us. It is of Him I write, and I write joyfully, thankfully, and with a full assurance, for I have tasted and seen for myself that He is gracious.

Elisha's story is like the garden of God in a barren land, an oasis in the desert. It is enlightening to the mind and delightful to the heart. God was there with Elisha, who was justly called "the man of God". He was never baffled. He was master of every situation and equal to every demand. All sorts of people came to him—kings, captains, lepers, great women and bankrupt widows, and they were blest in coming. He met friends and foes, good and bad, Israelite and Gentile, and freely bestowed his benefits upon them all, for the grace of God cannot be confined within any limits of any nation or class. His life was a joyous and overflowing life, for to give and forgive, to relieve and to bless, is God's own joy, and His chosen vessels share in it. Almost every phase of human need gave way to Elisha's ministry. There were limits with him, of course, for he was a failing man, a feeble vessel, and but the shadow of the coming, all-sufficient, and eternally glorious and perfect Saviour. Only Jesus could say, *"Come unto Me, all ye that labour and are heavy laden, and I will give you rest"* (Matthew 11:28). He has said it, and His deed is not less blessed than His word.

We notice that Elisha reached the place of his ministry through the river Jordan. God was with him when he came to that flood, and the waters were subdued before him, and not one drop of them wetted his sandalled feet. How different it was with Jesus when He came face to face with death, of which this Jordan was a figure. It was necessary that He should face death and endure it and pass through it if He was to be exalted to the Throne of Grace, "to be a Prince and a Saviour" there. He had to meet it in all its force. No miracle was wrought on His behalf in that great hour. No way was made through it for Him. Jordan overflowed all its banks when He came to it, and no helper could go through it with Him. In anticipation of it He breathed out His soul's deep agony in words that we cannot forget. "Now is My soul troubled; and what shall I say? Father, save Me from this hour: but for this cause came I to this hour. Father, glorify Thy Name." And again as He descended the banks of that river, and ere His feet touched its flowing waters, He prayed: "If it be possible, let this cup pass from Me." But it was not possible, and He had to cry, "The waters are come in unto My soul. I am come into deep waters, where the floods overflow Me" (Psalm 69:1-2). "Deep calleth unto deep at the noise of Thy waterspouts: all Thy waves and billows are gone over Me" (Psalm 42:7). His death was a necessity: apart from it "him that had the power of death, that is the Devil", could never have been annulled, and we could never have been delivered from his power. God's love could never have been known by us, for in no other way could it have been fully and righteously declared. But now "God commendeth His love toward us, in that while we were yet sinners, Christ died for us" (Romans 5:8). Apart from His

11

death our sins could not have been forgiven, we could not have been blest and saved, and there would have been no salvation and grace for sinners; for though our Lord would still have had a throne, high above all, for He is God, it would not have been, and could not have been, a throne of grace.

This is the Gospel that has been preached to us: "Christ died for our sins according to the Scriptures, and was buried and was raised again the third day, according to the Scriptures" (1 Corinthians 15:3, 4). And the glorious story of redeeming love goes farther than that: "Let all the house of Israel know assuredly, that God hath made this same Jesus, Whom ye have crucified, both Lord and Christ" (Acts 2:36). He became "obedient unto death, even the death of the Cross. Wherefore God also hath highly exalted Him, and given Him a Name that is above every name: that at the Name of Jesus every knee should bow ... and every tongue confess that Jesus Christ is Lord, to the glory of God the Father" (Philippians 2:8-11).

It is good for us to behold our Lord going down into the waters of death for us, as those sons of the prophets watched Elisha descend the banks of Jordan. It is good for us to behold Him coming out of death in resurrection, for of a truth a dead Saviour would have been no use to us. He would have been no Saviour at all if He had not come out of death, for "if Christ be not raised, ye are yet in your sins" (1 Corinthians 15:17). If death had overwhelmed and defeated Him, we might have wondered at the love that made Him die for us, but we should have mourned Him for ever, and no hope, no joy, no song would ever have dispelled our sorrow and gloom, and God would have lost His Son, and we should have had no Saviour, no Lord, no Leader, no One to Whom we could carry our needs and cares, no One to make us rich and overflowing with His grace.

But now is Christ risen from the dead; He, and not death has triumphed. He appeared to His disciples, and said to them, "Behold My hands and My feet, that it is I Myself" (Luke 24:39). And this appearance has been recorded for us in God's Holy Scriptures, that we might grasp its meaning by faith, and fall at the feet of Jesus risen from the dead, and cry with Thomas, "My Lord and my God!" (John 20:28).

Those young men who bowed before Elisha and owned him as their leader were right. It was God's will that they should acknowledge His chosen and anointed prophet in that way, and they were wise men when they did God's will. It is God's will that every tongue should confess Jesus as Lord. And "if thou shalt confess the Lord Jesus, and believe in thy heart that God hath raised Him from the dead, thou shalt be saved" (Romans 10:9). Those who deny the Lord that bought them bring upon themselves swift destruction, but those who bow before Him and confess Him and cleave to Him with purpose of heart are enriched by the grace of which He is the Administrator, for the great title and place of Lord, which is His now, not only means that He is set in the place of supreme authority, but that He is the Administrator of all God's grace to men. And it is through Him who is even at the right hand of God, Who also maketh intercession for us, that we are more than conquerors.

Salt in a New Cruse

*HOW THOSE WHO ARE LEARNING
THAT IN THEM DWELLS NO GOOD
THING, AND ARE ASKING, "WHO
SHALL DELIVER ME?" MAY BE
DELIVERED*

"He tarried at Jericho ... and the men of the city said unto Elisha, Behold, I pray thee, the situation of this city is pleasant, as my lord seeth: but *the water is naught, and the ground barren.* And he said, Bring me a new cruse, and put salt therein. And they brought it to him. And he went forth unto the spring of the waters, and cast the salt in there, and said, Thus saith the LORD, I have healed these waters; there shall not be from thence any more death or barren land. So the waters were healed unto this day, according to the saying of Elisha which he spake."

2 KINGS 2:18-22

Chapter 2
Salt in a New Cruse

It was a new era, and a happy one for Jericho, when Elisha went and abode there. Before it had been THE CITY OF DISAPPOINTMENT, for the situation of it was pleasant, but—and it was the men of the city that made the confession—the water was naught and the ground barren. From the time that the city had been founded on the ruins of its predecessor, a curse had been on it; its waters were tainted at the spring of them, and the land about it yielded only thorns for the labour of its people. It had not always been like that, for at one time it had been called "the city of the palm trees", but that was a matter of ancient history; and yet, with that fact on record, and the feeling that there was the possibility of better things in it, for its situation was pleasant, the inhabitants had hoped and laboured—but all in vain. It is more than likely that they had reached the point of despair when Elisha, the man of God, paid his memorable visit to them. And "he tarried there", and I am sure I am not far from the truth when I say that he did so because he desired to bless the city, and he dwelt among them until they were humble enough and honest enough to tell him the plight they were in.

Some of my readers have dwelt in the city of Jericho for a long time, expectation and disappointment have alternated in their experience. How eagerly they have hoped for better things, how sincerely they have vowed and resolved, how earnestly they have reached out after a better and more fruitful life than they have known, but they have missed it. Yet they feel that this ought not to be. Is not man's chief end to glorify God and to enjoy Him for ever, and to be supremely happy and a blessing to others in doing it? Then why are the waters of their lives so bitter, and the land of them so barren? Let us see if we can discover the reason and find the remedy.

First—and please do not be afraid of a little doctrine, for we cannot understand the situation without it—when man was created in the image and likeness of God, he was unquestionably "the city of the palm trees"; fresh and beautiful, and with unimpaired powers, he was capable of bringing forth fruit for God, and of being a channel of blessing to all. But he fell from that high estate. Just as the city of Jericho set itself in defiance against God's will, so Adam deliberately and wilfully turned away from God's commandment, and in that day of folly he fell as surely as did Jericho.

It was only natural that the sons of Adam should have endeavoured to recover their lost position and powers, but they have endeavoured without God, and their labours have been in vain. The sentence of death lies upon the race, as it lay upon Hiel, the Bethelite, who rebuilt Jericho and lost his eldest son when he laid the foundation and his youngest when he finished the gates of it, his whole family under death—"for by one man sin entered into the world, and death by sin; and so death passed upon all men, for that all have sinned."

In Paul's masterly letter to the Christians in Rome, he stresses this great doctrine in chapter 5, but when he comes to chapter 7, he shows how it works out in the life of the individual who has been awakened to what is right and desires to be what he feels God would have him be. What a history it is! What struggles! How poignant is the experience! We can almost hear the gasps and sobs of the man's soul as he is learning the bitter lesson that "the water is naught, and the land barren", until at last, realising that his best efforts are defeated and his struggles all useless, he cries: "O wretched man that I am, who shall deliver me from the body of this death?" And with such an experience as this in their souls and such a cry upon their lips, some of my readers have lived for a long time.

Now a word as to Elisha, so rightly called the man of God. He was a great contrast to Elijah. Elijah represented the law and pressed its demands upon the people. He came to tell them that the Lord, He is God! And to urge His just claims, and to tell them what they ought to be and do, and because they did not yield to God His rights and were not what they ought to be, condemnation and judgment always accompanied his ministry among them. But Elisha came, not demanding, but giving. He shewed out the goodness of God to a wretched people. He was a dispenser of grace and mercy, and all sorts of people were blest by him; nor did he turn away any who came to him acknowledging their need.

There was no hope for Israel in Elijah's ministry, and there is no hope in the law for us. It is "weak through the flesh", declares Paul, who knew it by experience. It cannot make us what we ought to be. It cannot change the barren land or sweeten the bitter waters; it can only expose and show up the barrenness and the bitterness, and condemn us. It has done so already; we lie under its sentence if we have invoked its aid. It is when we have reached that point in our soul-history, that we are ready for Elisha and the salt in the new cruse; we are ready for our Lord Jesus Christ, in His present glorious place as the Administrator of the grace of God. He is the Great Deliverer, Whose compassions reach down to men in their miseries.

I like the man who spoke for the delegation that waited on the prophet; there was a directness and brevity about his speech. He made no apology for their condition, and did not hide it; he stated the case in a few blunt words and waited. He did not even say what they would like the prophet to do. He felt that it was enough to tell him the need. It was enough, and his confidence in Elisha was met by an instant answer of grace and blessing. And, mark it well, it was Jericho, the one cursed city in the land, that got the blessing. Elijah had been to that city, and left it as he found it, and the inhabitants of it do not seem to have cared to appeal to him. But while Elisha tarried among them they must have been encouraged to approach him by his words and ways. He was the man, surely, to whom they could go, for he seemed so accessible, so sympathetic, so attractive.

There are no more blessed words in the Bible than those in John 1:14-17: "And the Word was made flesh, and dwelt among us ... full of grace and truth ... and of His fulness have all we received, and grace for (upon) grace. For the law came by Moses, but grace and truth came by (subsist in) Jesus Christ." Now, Jesus was Jehovah, Elisha's Lord, and whatever grace there was in Elisha was but as the light of the moon that is caught by it and reflected from the soon-to-rise sun. Jesus was the true Light, He was the Sun.

How wonderful was the love that brought Him down to us and to tarry with us in the barren lives and world in which we lived, not to demand from us and force the claims of the law upon us, or to condemn us for our iniquities and sins, but to save us. "For God sent not His Son into the world to condemn the world, but that the world through Him might be saved" (John 3:17). He came in grace; He was full of it. He came to give; we have no need to listen to another talking of Him in order to learn this, for He has told us Himself, "If thou knewest the gift of God, and who it is that saith to thee, Give Me to drink, thou wouldest have asked of Him, and He would have given thee living water" (John 4:10). "Jesus stood and cried, saying, If any man thirst, let him come unto Me, and drink. He that believeth on Me, as the Scripture hath said, out of his belly shall flow rivers of living water" (John 7:37, 38). He came with the new cruse, which was grace. The truth in the old cruse, which was the law, and which came by Moses, could only condemn us, for the blessings of which it did speak could only be gained and held by absolute and continual obedience to its commands, and its curse rested upon all who continued not in all things that were written in it to do them; but the truth in the new cruse brought nothing but blessing, for it was the declaration that God is love, and that His love was bent upon blessing men.

No illustration, not even those that are divinely given, can nearly equal the truth, and these Old Testament stories were but the shadows of good things to come, and not the very image of them. The good things have come now, the substance has appeared, and that substance is Christ. He has done for us what Elisha never could have done for those men of Jericho, for "He hath redeemed us from the curse of the law, being made a curse for us: for it is written, cursed is every one that hangeth on a tree" (Galatians 3:13). How great was the love that moved Him thus! And as we meditate on such a statement of the truth as this, do not we feel constrained to say, "I am crucified with Christ: nevertheless I live; yet not I, but Christ liveth in me: and the life which I now live in the flesh I live by the faith of the Son of God, WHO LOVED ME AND GAVE HIM-SELF FOR ME" (Galatians 2:20). And again, "For what the law could not do, in that it was weak through the flesh, God sending His own Son in the likeness of sinful flesh, and for sin, condemned sin in the flesh", and this happened that there might be no more "death or barren land", but that "the righteousness of the law might be fulfilled in us, who walk not after the flesh, but after the Spirit" (Romans 8:3, 4).

Yes, the truth (which is salt indeed) as to what we are and what God is, has been brought to us in surpassing grace. It is "the grace of God that brings salvation" (Titus 2:11); and as it comes into our souls we realise our own barrenness, and how utterly beyond all hope of improvement the flesh is, for in it good does not dwell, and we turn from it and cast ourselves completely upon Christ.

Then the truth that we have often read in the Word, but never received into our souls, becomes at last living to us and in us. The law of the Spirit of Life in Christ Jesus makes us free from the law of sin and death (Romans 8:2), and now deliverance from barrenness and death lies in cultivating the flesh no more, but in honestly confessing that there is no good thing in it, and in turning to Christ Who bore its condemnation for us when He was made a sacrifice for sin. We know that He was raised again from the dead, for it is part of the truth of the Gospel which we have believed, and for us this means justification from all our offences (Romans 4:25). It is grace that has justified us from the guilty past, but upon this absolutely sure and righteous basis, so that the question of our guilt will never be raised again. And that same grace transfers us from the old Adam life that lies under condemnation and death, and could bring forth no fruit, to Christ, our risen Saviour, and it is thus that where sin abounded grace does much more abound (Romans 5:20), that now being made free from sin, and having become the servants to God, we might have our fruit unto holiness, and the end everlasting life (Romans 6:22).

But that is not all, for we read: "It is Christ that died, yea, rather, that is risen again, Who is even at the right hand of God, Who also maketh intercession for us" (Romans 8:34). He died that we might be justified; He lives and intercedes that we might live as justified people. But it is all Himself—the truth is in Jesus. It has come to us in wonderful grace, and it is this that changes everything and enables us to close the chapter of earnest resolutions and bitter disappointments, and open the new one of perfect rest in our Lord Jesus Christ and fruitfulness to God, His Father, and blessing to others.

And the city of Jericho became "the city of the palm trees" once more (2 Chronicles 28:15), and there the naked were clothed and the hungry were fed, and the feeble were helped, and there long separated brethren were united again, and the people were obedient to the Word of God. So it shall be with every one of us who turn wholly to the Lord and cleave to Him with purpose of heart. The grace that began with our salvation will not fail us; it is sufficient for our whole lives in every phase of them. And while it teaches us to live soberly, righteously, and godly in this present evil world, it assures us of a new life of liberty, fruitfulness, and blessing. And such a life must be as happy as it is new.

"Bring Me a Minstrel"

HOW DISCORDANT LIVES MAY BE
PUT INTO TUNE

"So the king of Israel went, and the king of Judah, and the king of Edom; and they fetched a compass of seven days' journey: and there was no water for the host, and for the cattle that followed them. And the king of Israel said, Alas! that the LORD hath called these three kings together, to deliver them into the hand of Moab! But Jehoshaphat said, Is there not here a prophet of the Lord, that we may inquire of the LORD by him? And one of the king of Israel's servants answered and said, Here is Elisha, the son of Shaphat, which poured water on the hands of Elijah. And Jehoshaphat said, The Word of the LORD is with him. So the king of Israel and Jehoshaphat and the king of Edom went down to him. And Elisha said unto the king of Israel, What have I to do with thee? Get thee to the prophets of thy father, and to the prophets of thy mother. And the king of Israel said unto him. Nay; for the LORD hath called these three kings together, to deliver them into the hand of Moab. And Elisha said, As the LORD of hosts liveth, before Whom I stand, surely, were it not that I regard the presence of Jehoshaphat the king of Judah, I would not look toward thee, nor see thee. But now bring me a minstrel. And it came to pass, when the minstrel played, the hand of the LORD came upon him."

2 KINGS 3:9-15

Chapter 3
"Bring Me a Minstrel"

Three kings: the heathen Edomite, the apostate Jehoram, and the godly Jehoshaphat: a strange alliance this, an alliance that pleased the Devil well, but that grieved the God of Abraham to the heart. No wonder that disaster, swift and sure, followed upon the campaign, for how could that prosper in which a child of God took part, which had been conceived and carried into execution without any reference to the Lord, and in association with those who hated Him?

So these kings went, and "they fetched a compass of seven days' journey: and there was no water for the host"; and it seemed as though the fears of Israel's monarch were to be realised. "Alas! that the Lord hath called these three kings together to deliver them into the hand of Moab."

Then turned the thoughts of Jehoshaphat to Jehovah; then desired he to know, for the first time in that ill-starred venture, what the Lord would say; and, wonderful mercy! even while he cried out for a prophet, Elisha, the man of God, stood before him.

Mark well this fact, for it will be a help to us in our exercises as we proceed with our subject. We learn from it, as from many other incidents in the Word, that the thoughts of God's saints never turn to Him in vain; no matter what their circumstances, or the cause of them. He is ready to answer even while they call. "They cry unto the Lord in their trouble, and He bringeth them out of all their distresses" (Psalm 107:28). How great are the compassions of our God!

The discord of that unholy alliance distressed the prophet; it jarred upon his spirit, which had been tuned in communion with God, and he would have said nothing at all but for the fact that a saint of God in trouble stood before him. But ere he could speak the word of the Lord, the minstrel had to be brought. Harmony must take the place of discord.

Let us turn from the picture to the lesson. There are thousands of Christians bemoaning the lack of blessing. In spite of apparent diligent search, they do not find the waters of refreshment; their spiritual life is a desert, like unto "the wilderness of Edom". Their service and religious exercises have become a matter of routine; and in some cases a burden: and they wonder why!

In the majority of cases the reason is not far to seek; it is association with the world, unholy alliance with the godless for the pursuit of things which satisfy ungodly desires. *In every case it is because the life is out of harmony with God.*

A minstrel is needed, one who can take up the life and tune the chords of it, so that the discordant present may give place to the melody of a life in subjection to God. The Holy Ghost is the blessed Minstrel Who has come from Heaven with this purpose in view. But how easily and soon do Christians forget that the Holy Spirit of God dwells within them, how easily and soon do the vain things of this world and of man attract the mind and heart; then the heavenly Minstrel is grieved, the life drops out of harmony with God, and the waters neither spring up in praise nor flow out in blessing.

Christ is the key to which every note in our lives must be pitched, and we must know, and the Holy Ghost is here to teach us, where Christ is, and why He is there. He is on the Throne, crowns of God's approval shine upon His glorious head, and we gladly own the righteousness of this. But have we realised why He is there? He is there, of course, because the Father delights to honour Him; He is there, of course, because He is abundantly worthy of that place of pre-eminent glory; He is there, of course, because none other place in the universe but the right hand of the Majesty on high is suitable to the One Who fully carried out the will of God in making expiation for sin. But He is also there because the world rejected Him; He is there because the world cast Him out, nailing Him to a cross of shame. His exaltation in Heaven is God's glorious answer to the ignominy that was awarded Him by a world that hated Him.

Let us contemplate this great and solemn truth. Let us contemplate it in the presence of God, and give place in our souls for its meaning—for the meaning of *the Cross of Christ*. In Paul the Apostle we see a man in whose life the Cross held sway. "God forbid", said he, "that I should glory, save in the Cross of our Lord Jesus Christ, by which the world is crucified unto me, and I unto the world" (Galatians 6:14). He could not play the traitor to his Lord by accepting honour from the world that crucified Him. And if he remained in it, it was only that he might win the hearts of men for the One Who filled his own with joy and worship, so that they might be, even as he was, "not of this world", even as Christ was not of it. Let us take this same road, and say to the One Who loved us and gave Himself for us:

> *"I bind Thy shame upon my brow,*
> *Earth's only crown for me. "*

If our lives are concordant to the world, they are discordant to the God and Father of our Lord Jesus Christ; and if they are discordant to God, everything else must be wrong. The Scripture, which carries with it all the authority of God, shows clearly that there can be no harmony between God and the world, and it will allow no compromise with the world on the part of those who are God's. Paul asks: "What fellowship hath righteousness with unrighteousness? and what communion hath light with darkness? and what concord hath Christ with Belial? or what part hath he that believeth with an infidel? ... Wherefore come out from among them and be ye separate, saith the Lord, and touch not the unclean thing" (2 Corinthians 6:14-17). John tells us that "if any man love the world, the love of the Father is not in him" (1 John 2:15). James is stronger than all, for he says, "Ye adulterers and adulteresses, know ye not that the friendship of the world is enmity against God? Whosoever then will be a friend of the world is the enemy of God" (James 4:4). These words need no comment, they are self-explanatory, and if by any subtle reasoning by "the god of this world", we have been led into compromise with the world, our unfaithfulness in this respect is the cause of the low spiritual tone in the soul. All such unfaithfulness is sin, and the way of restoration is by confession. "If we confess our sins, He is faithful and just to forgive us our sins, and to cleanse us from all unrighteousness" (1 John 1: 9).

Other things than worldliness also spoil the music and grieve the Holy Spirit—selfish living, hard thoughts and harsh words about our fellow-Christians, an unforgiving spirit, indifference to the claims of Christ. Each one knows for himself wherein he fails, and where failure is there repentance must be. But how blessed it is to know that the Lord stands near us in unchanging love.

> *"How sweet 'tis to discover,*
> *If clouds have dimmed my sight,*
> *When passed, Eternal Lover,*
> *Towards me as e'er Thou'rt bright."*

But He will have truth in the inward parts, and there must be the confessing and the forsaking of what is not of God.

Where there is confession there will be restoration to communion with God, and the Holy Ghost will bring us into harmony with God by making Christ all in all to us. If He has His way with us He will bring us into full accord with Christ in glory, and keep us right as regards the world, and make every chord in our being sound out its full-souled praise to God.

And every word of God will then be sweet to us, and the waters of refreshing will flow into our souls from the Living Fountain of all good, making our lives to yield fruit for God, and blessing for men.

"Make this Valley full of Ditches"

HOW THOSE WHO LONG FOR THE BLESSING OF GOD MAY SECURE IT

"And he said, Thus saith the LORD, Make this valley full of ditches. For thus saith the LORD, Ye shall not see wind, neither shall ye see rain; yet that valley shall be filled with water, that ye may drink, both ye, and your cattle, and your beasts. And this is but a light thing in the sight of the LORD: He will deliver the Moabites also into your hand. And ye shall smite every fenced city, and every choice city, and shall fell every great tree, and stop all wells of water, and mar every good piece of land with stones. And it came to pass in the morning when the meat offering was offered, that, behold, there came water by the way of Edom, and the country was filled with water."

2 KINGS 3:16-20

Chapter 4
"Make this Valley full of Ditches"

THAT great army in the wilderness of Edom was in most desperate peril. They had no water, and their enemies the Moabites were gathering to the attack. No water meant disaster, defeat, destruction. They could gain no victory without water, and for it they had searched without success. God only could supply it; they had no hope but in Him. But they were a backslidden people. Would God think of them? Yes, He pitied them, and as He had often intervened for their deliverance before, so now through His prophet, who spoke for Him, He gave then what they needed, and they returned from the fight victorious and enriched.

That waterless army is a vivid picture of a vast number of those who profess to be God's people to-day—of Christendom, in fact—they have no water, and without water—the living water in this case—they are a defeated people, for no waterless Christian ever overcame the Moabite, who is the outstanding figure in the Old Testament of the evil flesh with its self-pleasing and godless desires.

It is as plain as can be that this waterless and defeated condition is the prevalent condition, and the tragedy is ten times worse, because so few seem to feel it. There is no living water in Ritualism, of course, yet multitudes are turning to it in the hope of finding some soul-satisfaction; it cannot give that; it may gratify the senses, but it most surely deadens the conscience, for it fills the mind with rites and ceremonies instead of God. And Modernism is the way of the wilderness in which there are no springs; it is worse, if that were possible, than Ritualism, for it puffs up the mind with a barren pride, and robs men of what sense of need they have, and makes them despise the Gospel of the grace of God. It is a broad road that leads to destruction, and many there are that go in it. But there are others who turn away from these popular phases of present-day religion, who are orthodox, and have true faith, and yet have no freshness or spiritual vigour in their lives. Like the God-fearing Jehoshaphat, they have been lured into the wilderness of Edom, they are backsliders, and they know it and feel it.

There are others who are not exactly backsliders, who are not happy. Their faith in Christ has not brought them the liberty and victory and joy of which the Bible speaks. The fact is, they have not come into the fulness of the blessing that there is in Christ for them. It is to these joyless Christians that I address my words, and what I have to say will help them if they will hear, no matter what the cause of their unsatisfactory and unsatisfied lives may be.

Elisha promised that thirst-stricken host abundance of water, and Jesus our Lord offers to you an overflowing abundance of Living Water. There are things said about Him by those who knew Him that are very wonderful. Take the words of the beloved disciple in the first chapter of his Gospel: "The Word was made flesh and dwelt among us, full of grace and truth ... and of His fulness have all we received and grace *upon* grace" (John 1:14, 16). The thought is of the mighty sea flowing in wave upon wave upon the shore, filling every inlet and crevice and cave. Is the grace of Jesus like that? It must be, for so this Holy Ghost-inspired man described it, and he described what he had known in his own experience. But hear the Lord's own words: "He that drinketh of the water that I shall give him shall never thirst; but the water that I shall give him shall be in him a well of water springing up into everlasting life" (John 4:14). And again: "If any man thirst, let him come unto Me and drink. He that believeth on Me, as the Scripture hath said, out of his belly shall flow rivers of living water" (John 7:37, 38). Am I wrong in describing these sayings as amongst the most arresting and magnificent that God has ever made to men? It is not here a question of the forgiveness of sins, great as that grace is, nor of Heaven, when life on earth is done; we bless Him for that, but it is the more abundant life, springing up in joyous worship and flowing out in constant good. Is it possible? It *must* be so, for the words are the words of Jesus, and He is God, Who cannot lie.

It is the fulness flowing in to the life, wave after wave, and flowing out again in rivers; flowing in for continual blessing, flowing out in victorious life and service, flowing into a hitherto barren life, and flowing out into a weary, polluted, sin-burdened and Devil-oppressed world, and healing, comforting, fertilising wherever it flows. I know your heart longs for it, it may be you feel that you must have it. May that feeling be deepened, for the deeper your desire the greater will be your satisfaction. But how can it be?

Turn again to our story. Said the man of God: "Make this valley full of ditches." It is clear that that meant make room for the water. It is not difficult to realise the stir that the prophet's command would make in that host. Not a man would be idle, every pick and spade would be busy, and everything that would hinder the flowing of the longed-for water would be removed. That is the secret. Are you ready to dig? First of all ponder the words of your Lord and Master. Do not let the fact that you have never realised the truth of them affect you. Your failure in the past and the failure of others does not alter the truth of them. There they stand in all their stupendous simplicity, describing what there is in Him for us, and what contact with Him will do for us. "This spake He of the Spirit, which they that believe on Him should receive: for the Holy Ghost was not yet given; because Jesus was not yet glorified" (John 7:39). He is glorified now, the highest place in Heaven has been given to Him Who died for us and rose again, hence there is no hindrance to the flowing of these waters on His side. The hindrance is on your side. In the Name of your Lord, and by the grace that He gives, arise and dig. Make the valley full of ditches. Make room for the blessing. Nay, in this case, make room for the Holy Spirit to work. If you have believed the Gospel of your salvation, the good news of Him Who died for your sins and was buried and rose again, you have no need to ask for the Spirit, for He has already sealed you, as saith the Scriptures (Ephesians 1:13, 14). But you must make room in your life for His work and the blessing that He brings.

It was in the valley that the digging had to be done. It is when a man descends from the mountain of his pride, and humbled before God, confesses his need, that he is ready to dig. You have longed for the blessing; have you longed for it enough to dig the ditches and to cast aside all that could hinder the flowing of the waters? You know what the hindrances are, and if you don't, God will show you, if you will go to Him with David's prayer on your lips, "Search me, O God, and know my heart: try me, and know my thoughts: and see if there be any wicked way in me, and lead me in the way everlasting" (Psalm 139:23, 24).

But it is not your digging that brings the water. All you can do only makes room for that which God has for you in Christ and it cannot be separated from Him. God has bound up the blessing of all men who are blest with the glory of His beloved Son, and no man, be he saint or sinner, will ever be blest apart from Him. For mark it well, *"It came to pass in the morning, when the meal offering was offered, that behold, there came water by the way of Edom, and the country was filled with water."* That morning oblation was a type of the preciousness of Christ to God. If offered in faith it represented the offerer's appreciation of Him, the Coming One. To take it out of the type and bring it down to present reality, it means that the excellency of the knowledge of Christ Jesus our Lord is a real thing to us. We delight in the One in Whom God delights.

And it is only as we delight in Christ that we are prepared to surrender things for Him, to dig the ditches. Philippians 2 very blessedly sets before us our Lord as the antitype of the morning oblation, and in chapter 3 Paul says: "What things were gain to me, those I counted loss for Christ. Yea, doubtless, and I count all things loss for the excellency of the knowledge of Christ Jesus, my Lord: for Whom I have suffered the loss of all things, and do count them but dung, that I may win Christ" (verses 7, 8). How thoroughly he had dug the ditches, and how great was the compensation.

The man who stands in any measure where Paul stood, into whose soul the waters have flowed, will certainly overcome the Moabite, for the flesh can have no power over the Christ-absorbed and Holy Ghost-filled man. He walks in the Spirit, and he does not fulfil the lusts of the flesh. He says, "Not I, but Christ." He is more than a conqueror through Him that loved him, and he becomes the open channel of blessing to others.

No longer will his life be like the way of the wilderness of Edom, but wherever he is the waters will flow, in home, office, or factory; in the Gospel service or Sunday school class, at home or abroad, in life and testimony, day by day and hour by hour, rivers of living water!

It is thus that Revival will come, whether in our lives as individual Christians, or in the Church generally, and in no other way. God does not withhold the blessing, the hindrance is not on His side, but on ours; we are so slow to make room for it, we cling so much to our thoughts and ways and importance, to self and self interests, and these are the hindrances. Let us make the valley full of ditches. In the Name of our Lord arise and dig!

"What hast thou in the House?"

HOW THOSE WHO ARE TROUBLED
ABOUT THEIR SINS MAY HAVE
PEACE WITH GOD

"Now there cried a certain woman of the wives of the sons of the prophets unto Elisha, saying, Thy servant my husband is dead: and thou knowest that thy servant did fear the LORD; and the creditor is come to take unto him my two sons to be bond-men. And Elisha said unto her. What shall I do for thee? Tell me, what has thou in the house? And she said, Thine handmaid hath not anything in the house, save a pot of oil. Then he said, Go, borrow thee vessels abroad of all thy neighbours, even empty vessels, borrow not a few. And when thou art come in, thou shalt shut the door upon thee and upon thy sons, and shalt pour out into all those vessels; and thou shalt set aside that which is full. So she went from him, and shut the door upon her and upon her sons, who brought the vessels to her; and she poured out. And it came to pass, when the vessels were full, that she said unto her son, Bring me yet a vessel. And he said unto her, There is not a vessel more. And the oil stayed. Then she came and told the man of God. And he said, Go, sell the oil, and pay thy debt, and live thou and thy children on the rest."

2 KINGS 4:1-7

Chapter 5
"What hast thou in the House?"

A moving story is this of the widow and the way that Elisha met her need. We see the need first of all, then the grace that met the need. It is a picture in which the dark background of the sinner's need throws into bright relief the wondrous grace that is in Christ for him. A widow in the Scriptures is a figure of perfect helplessness and an object for pity, and this widow was a bankrupt; her case was doubly sad, but it portrays the case of every sinner out of Christ. I want you to look at this picture, whoever you may be that know not the Saviour and His grace, and see yourselves in it. You are a bankrupt sinner, and you cannot relieve yourself of your liabilities, you are "without strength". The Lord Jesus Christ, Who always spoke the truth, propounded a parable in the Pharisee's house, in which He spoke of a certain creditor who had two debtors, who could pay him not a cent. God is that Creditor, and we are those debtors. You may not be the five hundred pence debtor, but a debtor you most surely are, and you have nothing to pay.

The widow awoke to her serious position when THE CREDITOR CAME TO PUT IN HIS CLAIM. Thank God, He, the Creditor, is not putting in His claim to-day. Instead, He is offering to relieve sinners of their debts, He is proclaiming forgiveness to all. "God was in Christ, reconciling the world unto Himself, (when He came into the world), not imputing their transgressions unto them, and hath committed unto us the word of reconciliation" (2 Corinthians 5:19). People in their pride refuse to own that they are sinners before God, they do not like to go down and confess the truth. They delude themselves with the thought that there is something in them that God can accept, and that they may be able to gain His favour by their works. The day is coming when they will be terribly undeceived, the scales will fall from their eyes, and they will see how they stand before God. When will that day be? It will be when the Creditor puts in His claim. I address myself to those whose eyes are still closed. You are drawing near to a terrible hour in your history. You say, What hour? The hour of your death. The clock of time is ticking out your days, and every swing of its ceaseless pendulum is bringing you nearer to that hour when you will step out of time into eternity. What is it that makes men who do not know God afraid of death? It is what comes after death. "After this the judgment." When you pass out of this world, you will meet God, and His judgment on your life. Some tell us that there is mercy after death, but God's Word does not say so. We believe in mercy with all our hearts, for God is rich in mercy, and He offers it to all—but not after death. "After death," God says, "the judgment" (Hebrews 9:27)—the Creditor will put in His claim then, for "every one of us must give an account of himself to God" (Romans 14:12). Then you who have refused to submit to God and own the truth about yourself will discover that you are bankrupt indeed, with nothing to pay. Then will it be justice—judgment without mercy!

This widow woman in her need turned to the man of God. There was one person in the land to whom she could go, and to him she went, and found that he was prepared most graciously to listen to her. So gracious was he that I can understand her telling him the whole story without reserve. He would encourage her to keep nothing back; the full amount of the debt, and how long it had been standing against her, and how it was contracted. He said to her, and there was grace in the words he uttered and the way he uttered them, "What shall I do for thee? Tell me, what hast thou in the house?"

Our hearts warm to the man of God as we read his words, but how shall I describe to you the grace of Jesus? I can tell you how He treated me. I came to Him as a needy sinner, and He made me feel that He was glad to see me. I felt that He was my Friend—the Friend of sinners, and that I could tell to Him what I could tell to no other. As He treated me, He will treat you. If you feel your need, go to Jesus, and you will find that He is the blessed Man of God, of Whom Elisha was but a feeble foreshadowing. You will find Him ready and able to take up your case and meet your utmost need.

Said Elisha to the woman, "What shall I do for thee? What hast thou in the house?" And she said, "Thine handmaid hath not anything in the house save a pot of oil." House-proud she may have been at one time, but piece by piece her household goods had gone, and now nothing was left but a pot of oil, of little or no value in her eyes. Yet that simple pot of oil, unheeded, unvalued, was all that was needed. It is even so with you. There is close at hand that which would have met your need long ago, if only you had turned to the Saviour—it is that of which the pot of oil speaks, as in a parable—it is THE GRACE OF GOD THAT BRINGETH SALVATION.

This was olive oil that was so near to the widow's hand, for the olive tree abounded in that land. Have you not read in the Psalms, words that could only be true of the Lord Jesus Christ: "I am like a green olive tree in the house of My God?" To obtain the oil from the olive tree its fruit must be crushed in the oil press and subjected to great heat. Before the precious oil of God's grace could flow for us, this blessed Person Who was the tender green olive tree growing in a dry and barren world had to be crushed in an unparalleled agony and sustain the fire of God's holy wrath against sin. He had to suffer beneath the stroke of God's justice when He became the sinner's substitute, for righteousness had to be satisfied, and only at the Cross of Christ do we see everlasting righteousness vindicated and satisfied. There He was made sin for us. He was delivered for our offences. He died for the ungodly. He paid the great price when He gave Himself for us, and as a result of His great sacrifice the grace of God is flowing freely for sinners to-day.

Then said the prophet of God, "Go, borrow thee vessels of all thy neighbours, EVEN EMPTY VESSELS—BORROW NOT A FEW, and bring them into the house, and shut the door upon thee and thy sons, and pour out into all those vessels." Away went the widow, believing the word of the prophet, and gathered into the house empty vessels, and when the house was full of them, and the doors shut, she took the oil, and to her astonishment it ran and poured and flowed, until every empty vessel was full. Those vessels were probably different in size, shape, and material—there would be among them some small and some large, some beautiful in shape and others rude and rough in appearance; some of costly material and others of no value at all; but they were all alike in this respect—they were all empty vessels. What is an empty vessel? An empty vessel is a vessel out of which you can get absolutely nothing, but into which you can put exactly what you please. And into such vessels as these the oil poured. Are you prepared to go to the Lord and tell Him that you are an empty vessel, that you have nothing to give Him, that you are a bankrupt sinner, with nothing to pay? Will you say to Him:

"I am an empty vessel,
Not one thought or look of love to Thee I ever brought,
Yet I may come, and come at once, to Thee,
With this, the empty sinner's plea, Thou lovest me!"

No two sinners are exactly alike as to external appearance, character, or circumstance; some are rich, others poor; some are learned, some ignorant; some are religious, and others profane; these things do not matter, but this does matter, they must be empty vessels. This is essential to blessing. I press it upon you, you must lift empty hands to God if you would have His blessing. You can pay nothing and do nothing on your own behalf.

"You have nought to plead,
Save God's rich grace
And your exceeding need."

The oil flowed and poured until all the vessels were full, and there was not a vessel left, and WHEN THE LAST VESSEL WAS FILLED, THE OIL STAYED. That is a serious consideration. If you refuse to take the place of an empty vessel before God, you will surely miss the blessing, for the day is coming when the grace of God will cease to flow, or you will be beyond the reach of it. In the New Testament we read that "the door was shut". Those who had got the oil in their vessels went in to the marriage feast, and the door was shut. Those who had not got the oil went to buy it, and they found that it could not be obtained. They were too late, for the saving grace of God, the oil no longer flowed, they had neglected this great salvation, and were shut out of the marriage feast.

> *"Make haste! make haste! the blessing is for thee;*
> *The cup of everlasting love is free."*

When all the vessels were filled, the widow hastened away to the man of God, and told him what had happened. What joy must have filled her soul, when Elisha said, "GO AND SELL THE OIL AND PAY THY DEBT." Was there sufficient oil to pay the debt? There was sufficient. Is there sufficient grace to clear away your debt? Is there forgiveness for you? Yes, even for you; for where sin abounds, grace doth much more abound. The grace of God is sufficient to pardon your sins and to justify a guilty sinner like you. God can justify you freely by His grace, through the redemption that is in Christ Jesus. Then you will look back on the dark past and say, "The debt is paid, the past is all wiped out. God Himself has nothing against me. He has justified even me."

In the 8th chapter of Romans we read: "There is therefore now no condemnation to them which are in Christ Jesus." If God justifies a man, he is justified, and cannot be condemned, for God's verdict must stand. He must have the last word about everything. Those who are justified are not so blessed because of what they are, nor because of what they have done, but because of what God is, and because of what Christ has done. It is what God is that is set forth in His great salvation. He is the God of all grace, and He has got a righteous basis for thus blessing men, and that basis is the redemption that is in Christ Jesus. The work of Christ has given God a right to justify those who believe in Jesus, and if you will believe in Jesus God will justify you. It is "to him that worketh not, but believeth on Him that justifieth the ungodly, his faith is counted to him for righteousness." Can you refuse to believe in a God like that? A God Whom we see set forth at Calvary?

But that is not all. The man of God said to the widow, "Pay thy debt, and LIVE THOU AND THY CHILDREN ON THE REST." There was a superabundance, enough to keep this woman and her children until the end of the story. So you will find it with the grace of God. The grace of God is not exhausted when it pardons our sins—nor when it justifies us. There is the rest of the grace, and it is at our disposal until the end.

The grace that is in our Lord Jesus Christ is sufficient for every need. There is no circumstance in which any of us can be found, allowed by the will of the Lord, but the grace of the Lord is sufficient. There is no circumstance into which any Christian can be led by his own folly, out of which the grace of God cannot bring blessing to him. There is grace to restore us when we fall, there is grace to keep us from falling.

Elisha said, "Live thou and thy children on the rest", and when the man of God said *live,* he meant it. To live means to enjoy life—and it is life that God wants us to enjoy. He wants us to live as those who have eternal life, to live as His children ought to live. He wants us to bask in the sunshine of His blessed love. God Himself is the source and fountain of life to us, and Christ is the way the waters flow. If we have received it and given Him thanks for it, now let us show our gratitude by still drawing upon His inexhaustible stores of grace, so that we may truly live, and show forth His praises, Who has called us out of darkness into His marvellous light.

A Chamber for the Man of God

HOW THE ABIDING PRESENCE OF
THE LORD MAY BE GAINED

"And it fell on a day that Elisha passed to Shunem, where was a great woman; and she constrained him to eat bread. And so it was, that as oft as he passed by, he turned in thither to eat bread. And she said to her husband, Behold, now, I perceive that this is an holy man of God, which passeth by us continually. Let us make a little chamber, I pray thee, on the wall; and let us set for him there a bed, and a table, and a stool, and a candlestick; and it shall be, when he cometh to us, that he shall turn in hither. And it fell on a day that he came thither, and he turned into the chamber, and lay there."

2 KINGS 4:8-11

Chapter 6
A Chamber for the Man of God

The figure changes; the once bankrupt widow, now forgiven and free, gives place to a great woman with great possessions. And this unfolds to us a great truth. Christians, we who were once bankrupt sinners, are now a great people through the grace of God. We are the children of God, by faith in Christ Jesus. I hope we are not great in our own eyes, and I hope that we do not desire to be great in the eyes of the world; yet we are great in the eyes of Heaven. Hear the words of Holy Scripture: "The Spirit itself beareth witness with our spirits that we are the children of God, and IF CHILDREN THEN HEIRS; HEIRS OF GOD, AND JOINT-HEIRS WITH CHRIST; if so be that we suffer with Him, that we may be also glorified together" (Romans 8:16, 17). No angel has so high a place as this, nor can any claim so great a destiny.

I saw crowds of people waiting in the streets the other day, and learnt that the king's son was expected to pass, and when he did appear he was given a respectful and loyal welcome by the crowds, and perfectly right—honour to whom honour—he is a great person in the land, and the people acknowledged it. As you and I walk in the streets nobody notices us; we have no honour in this world, for we are nobodies in its estimation; but the day is coming when we shall enter our own land, the golden gates of the Father's house will be thrown back for us, and in that day the angels of God will line the shining way and welcome us home—the sons of God brought to glory by redeeming blood. This is the dignity that God has put upon us; may our ways be consistent with it. Let us live as the children of God should, as those who have great resources and a great destiny.

We owe everything to our Lord, and it is right that we should consider Him and His desires. What does He desire? Above all things He wants our company. His love, so true and tender, can be satisfied with nothing less from us.

Notice in our picture that THE MAN OF GOD PASSED BY THE HOUSE OF THE GREAT WOMAN CONTINUALLY. It is thus that our Lord acts. He seeks for a place within our hearts and lives. And the Holy Ghost has come to take of the things of Christ and show them to us, and thus He passes by us continually to win a place for Himself in our hearts. It is thus that we see Him in Revelation 3: "Behold, I stand at the door and knock", He says. "If any man hear My voice and open the door, I will come in to him and will sup with him and he with Me." The man of God did not force himself upon this woman's hospitality, but when she constrained him he went in and ate bread with her. It has been said, and truly said, that "we get as much of the company of the Lord as we desire". If we *constrain* Him He will not deny us His company; it is this that His heart yearns for, and it is a joy to Him when a responsive yearning awakens in our hearts.

I gather that these occasional visits of Elisha to the Shunammite's house were wonderful times for her, insomuch that she determined to have him there not as an occasional visitor, but as one of her household, a constant guest. And we, have we not known seasons of joy, when we admitted the Lord to our hearts? In sorrow we have sought Him, and He has blest us with His own comfort; in times of depression He has cheered us, and turned our mourning into songs of praise. He has touched our hearts with His love, and we have been ashamed of our neglect of Him, but rejoiced in His grace that abides ever the same. These seasons may not have lasted long, but they were wonderful while they did last. He gave them to us that we might long after Him more, and do what this great woman did for Elisha.

She said to her husband, "Behold, now *I perceive that this is a holy man of God,* which passeth by us continually. Let us make a little chamber on the wall ... and it shall be when he cometh to us that he shall turn in thither." Her perception was right—she was a wise woman. Oh, that we may be all like her in regard to Christ; but if we are to be, as she prepared a chamber for Elisha, so we must prepare a chamber for Christ. The heart is the chamber—your heart, dear Christian. It may not be very large, but it may be the guest-chamber of the King of glory. But how can the heart be prepared for Him? Let us learn the lesson that the story of this wise woman teaches.

She was a practical, thorough kind of woman, and I have no doubt that the first thing she did was to use the broom and clear out the cobwebs that were hidden in the dark corners, and sweep out of the chamber all that was unsuited to the desired guest. Test yourself here, dear Christian. Are there lurking in your heart things that you cherish that keep the Lord out of it? Ah, if you do but see

Him passing by, and get one glimpse of His glory, these cherished things will be filth and rubbish to you; you will feel them to be out of place, occupying time and space that the Lord would fill, and you will want to be rid of them. Do you say, "I have tried often to give up habits and things that I know are wrong, but have only failed, until I have almost despaired?"

Yes, I know that experience, and I know what you need— a true sight of the Cross upon which Jesus gave Himself for you to redeem you from all that iniquity that holds you, and to purify you unto Himself, to be His own peculiar treasure. You need that backward look to the Cross, and then an upward look to the glory into which He has gone, and the Holy Ghost Who dwells in you can give you both, and the Holy Ghost will be the power within you to bring you into conformity to Christ. It is in the presence of the Cross of our Lord Jesus Christ and by the power of the Spirit that we are enabled to condemn and turn out of our lives what is contrary to Christ, and, best of all, and most needful of all, to judge and turn from sinful self.

The Lord Himself will come to our aid if we place ourselves without reserve in His hands, and we may take up David's words and say to Him, "Search me, O God, and know my thoughts, and see if there be any wicked way in me." Lord, take Thy candle and go through every chamber of my life from its topmost turret down to its deepest vault. Light up with Thine own light the dark recesses in it, and show me things as they appear to Thee!

Now comes the furnishing of the chamber. Into the one that she prepared for Elisha, the great woman put A BED, A TABLE, A STOOL, AND A CANDLESTICK. The bed is the place of rest. You remember the words, "Come unto Me, all ye that labour and are heavy laden, and I will give you rest. Take My yoke upon you and learn of Me; for I am meek and lowly in heart; and ye shall find rest to your souls" (Matthew 11:28, 29). The yoke of the Lord means submission to His holy will, and His will is good and perfect and acceptable. It is not against us but for us, and when we yield ourselves to it the inward conflict and restlessness give place to quietness and rest. And as we learn of Him Who is meek and lowly in heart, the envyings and jealousy and ambitions of men that make them fret and fume do not trouble us; we can leave ourselves and our concerns in God's hand, and in confidence in Him find rest. This is the first thing; we have no chamber fit for the Lord to dwell in if this is absent, but in such a heart He will find His pleasure.

Then follows the table, and this speaks of communion. "I will sup with him and he with Me", said the Lord. He desires to enter into our things, our joys and sorrows, for He loves us and is interested in us as our dearest and truest Friend, and He desires to bring to us His own comfort and grace in all that may cause us grief, but He would also lead us into His things, for He wants us to sup with Him, to have communion with Him in His things as His friends. A heart that is at rest from itself and consequently free to hold communion with Him is a heart that is delightful to Him.

The stool comes next, and we must not overlook this. Mary understood the need and blessedness of the stool, for she sat at Jesus' feet and heard His word, and we can only be maintained in communion with Him as we sit at His feet and learn of Him. The old restlessness will reassert itself if we neglect this; but as we sit at His feet we shall abide in Him and His words will abide in us, and we shall ask what we will, for hearing His word and speaking to Him in prayer go together. At His feet we learn of Him, and the more we know of Him the more we love Him, and He has said, "If any man love Me he will keep My words; and My Father will love him, and We will come to him and make Our abode with him" (John 14:23). The chamber will not be tenantless if we show our love to the Lord by hearing and keeping His word.

Then the candlestick will be there. Our bodies will be full of light, having no part dark; sincerity and truth will mark us, and we shall shine for Him Who dwells within our hearts. The light that has shone in will shine out.

Into this chamber swept and furnished the man of God came, and lay there, and the Shunammite was a happy and honoured woman. May the spiritual reality pictured in this Old Testament story be true in every one of our lives!

"Is it well with thee?"

*HOW BROKEN HEARTS MAY FIND
SOLACE AND BLESSING THROUGH
SORROW*

"And when the child was grown, it fell on a day, that he went out to his father to the reapers. And he said unto his father, My head, my head. And he said to a lad, Carry him to his mother. And when he had taken him and brought him to his mother, he sat on her knees till noon, and then died. And she went up, and laid him on the bed of the man of God, and shut the door upon him, and went out. And she called unto her husband, and said, Send me, I pray thee, one of the young men, and one of the asses, that I may run to the man of God, and come again. And he said, Wherefore wilt thou go to him to-day? it is neither new moon, nor sabbath. And she said, It shall be well. ... And when Elisha was come into the house, behold, the child was dead, and laid upon his bed. He went in therefore, and shut the door upon them twain, and prayed unto the LORD. And he went up, and lay upon the child, and put his mouth upon his mouth, and his eyes upon his eyes, and his hands upon his hands: and he stretched himself upon the child; and the flesh of the child waxed warm. Then he returned, and walked in the house to and fro; and went up, and stretched himself upon him: and the child sneezed seven times, and the child opened his eyes. And he called Gehazi, and said, Call this Shunammite. So he called her. And when she was come in unto him, he said, Take up thy son. Then she went in, and fell at his feet, and bowed herself to the ground, and took up her son, and went out."

2 KINGS 4:18-23 AND 32-37

Chapter 7
"Is it well with thee?"

SUNLIT hills and shady valleys have their place in the earth as well as fertile plains and sun-scorched deserts, and God has made it so, for He is the God of diversity, as all His works declare. And our lives are like that. They are not on one dead level, we have our ups and downs, our laughter and our tears, the hill-tops and the valleys, and sometimes the deep, dark gorges from which it seems impossible that the feet that tread them could ever emerge.

Some have strange views of life, warped and limited; they would restrict the laughter or restrain the tears; but it is legality that does the one, and pride that attempts the other; and legality is of the flesh, and pride is of the Devil. There are those who imagine that there is no joy in the Christian life, and others who wonder why there should be any sorrow in it. The faith of the one has never grasped the fact that God gives us all things richly to enjoy, the others do not understand that He watches us with a Father's unwearying eye, and may sometimes see that it is necessary to chasten and reprove us lest we revel in earthly good and despise or forget the deeper and eternal things, and drift away from Him Who is the Giver of all good.

See how these two things are figured for us in the experiences of the great woman of Shunem. She was a great woman, the lady of the manor, but she was morally great also, as was evident when she declined to ask for any honour for herself or her husband. "I dwell among mine own people", she said. She was a contented woman, and what could the King or the Captain of the host do for her? A contented person is morally great, and this all God's children should be. The popular notion is that he is great who has great possessions, but "a man's life consisteth not in the abundance of the things that he possesseth" (Luke 12:15), but "godliness with contentment is great gain" (1 Timothy 6:6). That man is godly who walks in the fear of God, and has the Lord abiding with him, as this woman had Elisha dwelling with her, and he only is contented and able to refuse the preferments and prizes of the world that attract so many but satisfy none.

But Elisha represented a great and giving God, Who will reward even a cup of cold water that is given to one of His servants, and this woman of Shunem had been exceedingly careful for His prophet's comfort, and recompensed she must be. So the one earthly joy that she lacked was given to her. In the course of time this childless woman embraced a son, God's gift to her. Did He intend her to enjoy His gift? Most certainly He did. How strange it is that people should imagine that God does not want them to be happy in the gifts He gives them! How poor is their knowledge of Him. I have met Christians who thought that it was God's will to check and thwart them, and to take good things from them lest they should enjoy them over much, and they have been afraid, because of this, to trust themselves and their treasures wholly to Him. They were not happy Christians, and were no testimony for Him.

How different from this false notion is the way the Bible speaks of God. There we read that He does good and showers His blessings upon us, filling our hearts with food and gladness (Acts 14:17). And it is undoubtedly His will that His children should enjoy those natural relationships that are His own ordination, if they are received with thanksgiving and sanctified by the Word of God and prayer (1 Timothy 4:4, 5).

We are sure that this woman's home at Shunem was a happy one, but as the years rolled by, did she become absorbed with her domestic happiness and less careful for the man of God? It seems almost wrong to suggest it, yet during those years while she watched the development of her son no visit of the man of God to her home is recorded, though his chamber and his bed were still there. One thing is certain, she had more lessons to learn, and these are recorded for our admonition. She had learnt that the man of God was better than her possessions, and that he could bring greater blessing into her life and home than ever she had known. She had learnt that if she delighted herself in the Lord, He would give her the desire of her heart (Psalm 37:4). Now she had to learn that God's representative was her one resource in sorrow, and in the grace and power of God greater than death. She had to walk in the shadows as she had walked in the sunshine, and discover that the man of God was the same in both. The heart that has learnt these things in regard to Christ has been enriched with a knowledge that far exceeds all earthly joy, and can say, as Paul said: "I have learned in whatsoever state I am, therewith to be content. … Both to abound and suffer need. I can do all things through Christ which strengtheneth me" (Philippians 4:11-13).

There is here a striking commentary on the transitoriness of the choicest things in this life. The child has grown, it was harvest time and noon when he died on his mother's knees. When the promise of that young life was brightest, in the fulness of the year when the earth yielded up her wealth to the sickle, and at the zenith of the day the blow fell, and the mother's arms, the mother's love could not protect her child from it. Death smote him, and in smiting him it smote her and broke her heart.

The story of the crashing of that great woman's hopes, and the sight of her sitting alone with her dead son in her arms, brings vividly home to us the fact that no circle or sphere beneath the sun is immune from sorrow, or impregnable to death. If we have not learnt this lesson, and what it means to us, either by a sore experience or in communion with God, we have not advanced far in our Christian knowledge, nor have we understood the greatness of our Saviour and the tenderness of His heart. Death is here. Do we know to whom to turn when we feel it? "Death has passed upon all men" (Romans 5:12). Do we know where life abides? Nothing we possess in the natural sphere of life can we retain. Are our affections set on things above, where Christ sitteth and where death can never come?

It is a sore lesson, but it must be learnt: death is here. It must be learnt either in communion with God or through such an experience as this woman passed through. Of every man it is true as regards himself that the outward man perisheth, and the most cherished object of a man's heart may at any moment be severed from him. He may stand up to resist the advancing foe, but death heeds him not. He may gather all his treasures and pour them out and pile them up, he may offer himself instead: it is useless, it avails him nothing; death cannot be beaten off or bribed, nor will he accept a substitute. Human love is impotent, baffled, beaten, when death claims what is devoted to it, and the unhearing ears, the closed, unseeing eyes, the still, unresponsive heart all witness to the completeness of the breach. What would we do if such an experience were ours?

Let us consider the ways of this great woman, for she was as great in her sorrow as she was in her prosperity and joy. First she laid her son upon the prophet's bed. What a burden she carried into that chamber, where the prophet had lived and lain. We see her enter it with bowed head and weeping eyes, bruised, buffeted, bewildered. Did she bow in lowly prayer there? I believe she did, for she came forth submissive and calm, with one word in her heart and lips with which to meet all questions: "It is well."

She knew that no one would understand her sorrow like the man of God, who had given her the joy that she had lost. She must go to him, and if she could bring him back to that chamber which was his, he would find her sorrow there. Ah, there are many hearts that were once filled with the joy of the presence of the Lord upon which now a great sorrow is laid. It may be the sorrow of departure from the Lord, or it may be something that answers to the sorrow of this bereaved mother. Anyhow, it is death, moral, spiritual, or actual death, and the cry of the heart is, "Restore unto me the joy of Thy salvation."

Her sorrow did not rob her of her decision of character, and indeed in this matter there was no time to be lost, and this is so in all matters of lost joy and blessing, for sorrow can harden as well as soften; indeed it will most surely harden if the presence and sympathy of the Lord are not known, and the spirit that becomes absorbed with sorrow becomes strangely dulled, insensitive, and self-centred. "I will rise *now* and go about the city in the streets, and in the broad ways will I seek him whom my soul loveth", said the bride in the Canticles who had been indifferent to her lover and had lost the joy of his company. "I will run to the man of God, and come again", was this woman's determined purpose, and to her servant she said "Drive, and go forward; slack not thy riding for me, except I bid thee."

Do not think that I am confounding two things that differ, that I am mixing up the sorrow of a heart bereaved by death, and the sorrow of a heart that once knew the joy of the Lord's presence. I am not. If the Man of God is not dwelling in the prepared chamber, if Christ is not in the heart, it matters little what the reason for it may be, the great necessity is to seek Him, to recall Him without delay. It was this that this woman was set upon. Her husband does not seem to have had any deep spiritual feeling or discernment. He could not understand what use the man of God could be on any day but the Sabbath, or perhaps at the new moon, like so many whose irksome religion is but a matter of form and ceremony, a one-day-a-week affair, and who have no consciousness of all that need that some of us feel of an every day acquaintance with our living Lord. Anyhow, this lady of Shunem had neither the heart nor the time to argue the point. Her relations with the man of God were not formal; she felt that none but he could understand her sorrow, and she must pour it out at his feet that day. Yet her haste was not the result of panic or hysteria, as her noble answer to her husband proved. What confidence she had in God and His prophet when she said, "It is well!"

The man of God saw her afar off, and we may be sure that the Lord knows well and sees the first move towards Himself on the part of any of His own, no matter how far off they may be from Him. From Elisha had been hidden the cause of her coming to him, but nothing is hidden from our living Lord. Blessed be His Name! As she had refused to discuss her sorrow with her unsympathetic husband, so now she refuses to discuss it with Gehazi. Her answer, "It is well", shewed how thoroughly she had realised that not the servant, but his master only, could meet her deep need. And so she bends at his feet and pours out her sorrow there. And she will not be diverted from him, even when it seemed as though Gehazi was commissioned to raise up the child. She must have the man of God. "As the Lord liveth, and as thy soul liveth, I will not leave thee", she says. His presence had become the one necessity of her life.

This is plainly the way for hearts, whether broken or backslidden. No mere servant will suffice. Only personal contact with Christ and His company will do. He must take afresh the place that was once His in the heart. He must deal with sorrow and sin. He is greater than both. In the power of the Lord, Elisha brought back the dead child to life again and gave him to his mother, and she bowed again before him, not now in sorrow but in glad worship to the God Whom he served.

It is not the Lord's way to restore the dead to life in these days. Those who die in the Lord are with Him, which is far better; but He can and does make life spring out of death for us. He can and does turn our greatest sorrows into our greatest blessings, but He does this by drawing near to us Himself, and filling up our empty hearts.

DELIVERING GRACE

"A Dearth in the Land"

*HOW THOSE WHO ARE TROUBLED
ABOUT IT MAY DISCOVER THE
REASON AND THE REMEDY*

"And Elisha came again to Gilgal; and there was a dearth in the land; and the sons of the prophets were sitting before him; and he said unto his servant, Set on the great pot, and seethe pottage for the sons of the prophets."

2 KINGS 4:38

Chapter 8
"A Dearth in the Land"

"A dearth in the land!" How that would please the Devil. For would not the godless nations that hated Israel say with scornful utterance: "Is that all the Jehovah in Whom you have boasted can do for you? You came to this land when it flowed with milk and honey, and behold it now, dry as a sunbaked or rainless desert, and you, the chosen people, beloved of the Lord, hungry and dying. Our gods are better than yours." But Israel only was to blame; they were suffering because they had broken the commandments of the Lord, and because they were suffering the Devil was delighted, the tender heart of God was grieved, and His Name was blasphemed among the Gentiles.

"A dearth in the land!" How often we hear the sad tale told by saints of God who mourn the fact that error has usurped the place of truth; that their souls are not fed as in former days; that when they ask for bread they are given the stones of man's vain imagination, stones that no power can turn into bread, but which are the Devil's imitation of it, his invention with which he mocks the craving of the soul. They read of the days when Christ was ministered in the power of the Holy Spirit, and the

churches edified; and when with hearts on fire the
Christians witnessed for Christ and looked and longed for
His Coming again. They can remember the time when
even their hearts were greatly cheered and made happy by
ministry which was according to the Word of God—
which in these days has become unpopular, and has been
superseded by that which feeds the fleshly mind, and by
amusements galore. For it is said: "Must we not provide
something bright and attractive for the people; must not
they have entertainment and recreation? And is not this
the Church's mission?" And the saints of God are suffering, and the heart of the Lord is grieved, and His Name
blasphemed by those who love Him not, for they say:
"Then has your Lord failed you? Is your Christianity
played out? Does it no longer satisfy? Then welcome to
our board. Let us cater for you. Eat of our fare, for it is
better than yours." And the world, the flesh, and the
Devil preside at the feast; and love to Christ grows cold,
and spirituality wanes, and Christian life is sickly and
ready to die; and the world, while it patronises and flatters
and smiles, can barely conceal its contempt of a seduced
and faithless Church.

It would be an easy matter to fill volumes with an exposure of this condition of things, but those for whom we
write do not need such an exposure; they know it and
deeply feel it, and some of them go from their Sunday
services to weep and pray before the Lord about it all. The
questions they are asking are: What is the cause of this
dearth in the land? and, Why are the people of God not
fed? and, Is there any remedy? These questions I desire to
answer.

This condition of things has undoubtedly resulted from
the fact that the professed followers of the Lord have left
their first love, and have grown indifferent to His Word

and careless as to His Name. Like Israel of old, they have become slack concerning His will. They have given ears to those who first questioned and then denied the Word of God, until they know not what God has spoken, or whether He has spoken at all; they have no guide for their feet and no lamp for their path. They are like a ship at sea without compass or chart, being driven by false winds to certain wreck. Moreover, they have broken down the barriers that separated them from the world that crucified their Lord, as Israel mixed herself with the nations, and the foul weeds that are native to the world have shed their seeds in the fair garden of the Lord, and now grow rankly there. Indifference to the Word of God and association with the world are the result of the loss of first love to the Lord, and are the great devastators, and they are most certainly some of the reasons for the wide-spread dearth.

Elisha came to Gilgal, and there the dearth was, and the sons of the prophets were hungry. Now Gilgal was the last place at which you would have looked for dearth. It was nigh to the city of the palm trees on the banks of the life-giving Jordan. It was there that the Israelites first celebrated the Passover feast, and ate the old corn of the land. It was a place of happy memories, and those sons of the prophets would know all about its history, and sadly recall the good days long since past.

What a change the presence of Elisha made to those sons of the prophets. He was sent to them because God pitied them in their poverty, and he carried to them grace and power enough to relieve them of all their necessities. It is because of this that I say he stands as a type of the Lord Jesus Christ. It is good to have the Lord Jesus Christ to turn to, for He is full of grace and truth, and all the treasures of wisdom and knowledge are hid in Him. No problem or difficulty, no circumstance or crisis in which either individual saint or company of Christians can find themselves, can be too great for Him. He is equal to every test, and His grace is all-sufficient. "In Him dwells all the fulness of the Godhead bodily" (Colossians 2:9). Wonderful, most blessedly wonderful, and for ever adorable Saviour! He stands near to meet to the uttermost the needs of all who turn wholly to Him.

There is one way, and only one, in which His grace and power and wisdom may be ours. It is at our disposal, at the disposal of every individual saint, and of every company of God's people the wide earth over. But we must turn to Him for it, and in turning to Him acknowledge Him as Lord. He must be supreme. Surely He has a right to be supreme in His Church. Did He not love it and give Himself for it, that He might "present it to Himself a glorious Church, not having spot or wrinkle or any such thing, but that it might be holy and without blame" (Ephesians 5:27)? Are not the saints of God bought with a price, a price that never can be priced—that precious Blood? And if so, has He not the right to control and command, to be absolute in the affections and ways of His people? Who will dare to challenge His right? And to whom shall He be accountable? And yet as Israel once cast Him out of His own vineyard, so now is He cast out by a large proportion of His professing Church. He stands outside a closed door, as at the Laodicean Church. His Word has not been kept, His Name has been denied. This is, above all things, the cause of the great dearth.

The only remedy is to go back to first things. "Thou hast left thy first love. ... Remember from whence thou art fallen, and repent and do the first works" (Revelation 2:4, 5). There must be a return to the beginning, and in the beginning Christ was everything. His will was paramount. He alone was "honoured, loved, adored".

Let the saints of God who mourn the dearth give the Lord His rightful place in their midst, and if any are in religious associations where this is impossible, let them at once and for ever sever themselves from those associations, let them do it for the glory of His Name, and for the good of their own souls. Let none be satisfied with anything short of the absolute assurance that He has the supreme place in the midst of their gathering together, that He controls and not men. Then shall they be able to count upon those mighty resources that dwell in Him, and He will sustain them in the freshness and vigour of true Christian life.

We may not expect things to be as great as they were in former days, but there is no reason why they should not be as bright. And yet they will not be small, for no grace that the Lord bestows, or blessing that His presence gives, can be small. *"Set on the GREAT pot, and seethe pottage for the sons of the prophets"*, said Elisha. They must be fed. So the Lord can feed His saints, as He fed Israel in the wilderness when He rained down bread from Heaven for them. Look not to men of learning, lean not upon the servants of the Lord, let not your hope be in conferences, conventions, or Bible schools, but turn directly and completely to Him, the living Lord, who nourishes and cherishes His Church. Own His supremacy, and do His will simply and whole-heartedly, and leave every difficulty and all the consequences in perfect trust to Him.

"There is Death in the Pot"

*HOW CHRISTIANS AFFECT ONE
ANOTHER, AND WHAT TO DO
WHEN MANY SUFFER*

"And one went out into the field to gather herbs, and found a wild vine, and gathered thereof wild gourds his lap full, and came and shred them into the pot of pottage: for they knew them not. So they poured out for the men to eat. And it came to pass, as they were eating of the pottage, that they cried out, and said, O thou man of God, there is death in the pot. And they could not eat thereof."

2 KINGS 4:39, 40

Chapter 9
"There is Death in the Pot"

WHEN we go back to the beginning, we learn that the first thing in Christianity is the acknowledgment of the lordship and headship of Christ, and then, that believers, indwelt by the Holy Spirit and forming Christ's body, are necessary to each other; that they are all dependent one upon another, and that each contributes to the prosperity or harm of the whole. This truth is solemnly taught in 1 Corinthians 12:12-27. The help we render to each other is also most blessedly shown in Ephesians 4, the chapter in which the Lord's glorious supremacy over all things is declared. We read there: "But speaking the truth in love, may grow up into Him in all things, which is the Head, even Christ, from which the whole Body fitly joined together and compacted by that which every joint supplieth, according to the effectual working in the measure of every part, maketh increase of the Body UNTO THE EDIFYING OF ITSELF IN LOVE" (verses 15, 16).

The harm we may do to each other is illustrated in our story. They went out, these sons of the prophets, to gather herbs for the meal that Elisha had commanded. And one gathered wild gourds—his lap full—and came and shred them into the pot of pottage. His ignorance and folly almost resulted in the whole company being poisoned. There was death in the pot.

It was from a wild vine that he gathered his gourds, from a plant that had not come under cultivation—fit figure of the evil flesh. Of it we read: "The carnal (fleshly) mind is enmity against God; for it is not subject to the law of God, neither indeed can be" (Romans 8:7). It is that which has not and will not come under God's cultivation. And it always brings forth death and corruption, "for to be carnally minded is death" (Romans 8:6), and "he that soweth to his flesh shall of the flesh reap corruption" (Galatians 6:8).

Now, every believer is either walking in the Spirit or in the flesh; each one is pursuing the things of the Spirit or the things of the flesh, and whether we will or not, what we are, and how we live, and what we pursue, and that of which the heart is full affects all with whom we associate.

Suppose by way of illustration that envious feelings or a hard and unforgiving spirit is allowed or cultivated in the heart of any believer towards any of his brethren; or suppose one brother becomes jealous of another because he seems to have more honour than himself—these are bitter roots from which will spring "hatred, variance, emulations, wrath, and strife"—works of the flesh, and most deadly in their effects wherever they show themselves. How often have we seen happy Christian companies blighted and broken by "bitterness, wrath, anger, clamour, and evil speaking"; or as a result of one or more who ought to have served all in love, lording it over the Lord's heritage. Our associations with all the saints of God is a Divinely formed association, and we must not, we cannot ignore it. The spiritual prosperity of one is a help to all, and the works of the flesh in any means harm to all. We can no longer live as though we alone are affected by our living, "for if one member suffer, all the members suffer with it".

It was a happy thing for those sons of the prophets that Elisha was at hand, and that they had sufficient wisdom to refer the case to him. It is a most blessed and comforting thing to know that we may cry to the Lord, even when things are at their worst. He is our resource when death instead of life is in the pot. How different would things have been in the Church of God if the saints of God had had enough wisdom to do this, instead of trying themselves to put things right when they have gone wrong. How many a disaster might have been averted if instead of officious meddling there had been a lowly and brokenhearted crying to the Lord, if that which has proved beyond our skill to put right had been simply carried to Him; if we had said to the Lord, as the sons of the prophets said to Elisha, "O thou man of God, there is death in the pot."

There has been much failure in this respect, but He fails not, and we may count upon His deep and tender interest in His own, and counting upon this we shall not be disappointed. Moreover, He has the means where by the sorrow may be turned into joy, and spiritual health recovered to those who are sick.

"Then Bring Meal"

*HOW THE WORKS OF THE
FLESH ARE REBUKED, AND
HOW LIFE MAY TAKE THE
PLACE OF DEATH*

"And one went out into the field to gather herbs, and found a wild vine, and gathered thereof wild gourds his lap full, and came and shred them into the pot of pottage: for they knew them not. So they poured out for the men to eat. And it came to pass, as they were eating of the pottage, that they cried out and said, O thou man of God, there is death in the pot. And they could not eat thereof. But he said, Then bring meal. And he cast it into the pot; and he said, Pour out for the people that they may eat. And there was no harm in the pot."

2 KINGS 4:39-41

Chapter 10
"Then Bring Meal"

IT is so easy for us to think that we have only ourselves to please, and that we can do as we choose without regard to any other person. It is upon this most pernicious principle that the evil flesh that is within us acts, and it is thus that it serves the law of sin, for it is not only indifferent to the welfare of others, but it is also insubject to God. It is enmity against God; "for it is not subject to the law of God, neither indeed can be" (Romans 8:7). As we have already shown, the flesh is like the wild vine from which one of these ignorant sons of the prophets gathered wild gourds his lap full; if we tolerate or cultivate it, our laps will also be filled with sorrow and shame of its deadly fruits. And how terrible these fruits are! Some of them are enumerated in Galatians 5:19-21: "Adultery, fornication, uncleanness, lasciviousness, idolatry, witchcraft, hatred, variance, emulations, wrath, strife, seditions, heresies, envyings, murders, drunkenness, revellings, and the like." These things may not all appear equally heinous in our sight, but they are all the works of the flesh. Yes, variance, strife, and envyings are as truly works of the flesh as adultery, heresies, and murder. Corruption and death always follow in their wake, not only for the individual who gathers any one of them, and who, to change the figure of that most solemn one given by the Holy Ghost, must reap what he has sown, for God is not mocked (Galatians 6:7); but for many others also, who are associated with him as a member of Christ's Body. It is because this is so that we are exhorted to "follow peace with all men, and HOLINESS, without which no man shall see the Lord; looking diligently, lest any man fail of the grace of God; lest any root of bitterness springing up trouble you, AND THEREBY MANY BE DEFILED" (Hebrews 12:14, 15).

These sons of the prophets had they all been wise might have had the honour of contributing to the common good, but, through the ignorance of one and the folly of all, the meal that was intended for their nourishment threatened to do incalculable harm to every one of them. They brought in the poison and spoilt the feast, but they had no antidote for the harm that they had done. But at this point their wisdom returned to them, and they cried to Elisha, the man of God, and in doing this they laid their distress down in the presence of the power of God, which worked through him on their behalf.

Here is clearly indicated for us the way of wisdom in times of difficulty and sorrow. The Lord is our resource in every trouble. If we think of the responsibility of the saints of God to maintain the truth of God and to edify one another, these days are not better than any that have gone before. From the beginning and throughout the centuries carnality and failure have marked the Church's course. If the Church's history were written for us by the finger of God, what sad reading it would be. There have been times when the flesh has broken out outrageously, shocking even the natural conscience, but this, whenever and wherever it happens, is but a symptom of the general condition; fruit of the wild vine allowed to flourish in the very garden of God, and the common shame of all. We ought to have learned lessons from the past, but history repeats itself in our day, and our failure is less excusable than any that has gone before.

Yet the Lord has not changed, and He cannot fail. He has always been the resource of His saints when they have fallen upon evil days, and He is to-day. But the failure must be owned and the need confessed, and this means the humbling of our pride. We have often thought, when we felt that there was death in the pot, that we, by the application of some so-called principle in which we have boasted, could turn it into life; that we could straighten and correct that which was crooked and wrong by some ecclesiastical action of our own devising, perhaps; and it was often flesh correcting flesh, because it was not the peculiar kind of flesh that we favoured; and confusion has been made worse confounded and the evil increased ten-fold. We have saved ourselves, probably from the deep heart-searching that should have been ours, and preserved our pride and boasting, but have failed to reach the root, and have it all out and confessed and judged. May the Lord give us grace to feel this if it is so, and to confess it so that we may be cleansed from all unrighteousness, and may He preserve us from growing indifferent to the condition of things amongst His saints; and may we never fall into that fatalistic state of mind which says, "What is, must be; the Lord has allowed it, there is no remedy." May we be honest enough to make no attempt to hide our need from the eyes of the Lord, but instead, lay it all before Him, and say, as we feel it deeply and with tears, "Oh, Thou Man of God, there is death in the pot."

Elisha's remedy is not far to seek, for "he said, *Then bring meal.* And he cast it into the pot, and he said, Pour out for the people, that they may eat. And there was no harm in the pot." We have no wish to be fanciful in our application of this story to our present need, but it strikes us as being remarkable that Elisha called for meal and used it as the means of healing the pottage, and not salt as in the case of the waters of Jericho (2 Kings 2). And our thoughts are carried back to the Levitical offerings, one of which was the meat or meal offering (Leviticus 2). This offering was made of fine flour, and typified the life of the Lord Jesus here upon earth.

Every heavenly grace shone out in perfection in Him in manhood, for He was everything that the heart of God desired that man should be. But there are two traits that seem to be specially made prominent by the Holy Ghost for our help: they are His humility and obedience. They are set before us in the wonderful passage in Philippians 2: "Let this mind be in you, which was also in Christ Jesus: Who being in the form of God, thought it not robbery to be equal with God; but made Himself of no reputation, and took upon Him the form of a servant, and was made in the likeness of men: and being found in fashion as a man, He humbled Himself, and became obedient unto death, even the death of the Cross" (verses 5-8).

This is Christ as the meal offering, and He is presented to us in this character that we might admire, adore, and imitate. Think of His humility:

> *"Heaven's arches rang as the angels sang,*
> *Proclaiming His royal degree:*
> *But of lowly birth came the Lord to earth,*
> *And in great humility."*

Though He were in His own Person the everlasting God, yet He did not disdain the Virgin's womb and that lowly birth in the stable at Bethlehem. Though He were Lord of all, He accepted without resentment the despising of the people, and continued unweariedly to serve them. When His disciples contended who amongst them should be greatest of all, He, their Lord and Master, bent low to wash their feet. He sought no honour, no name for Himself; His joy was to do His Father's will, and to serve the weakest and the worst. And this path led only to the Cross, with its degradation and unparalleled shame. He knew from the beginning that this would be the end, yet He murmured not. It was obedience that led Him along that road, but His humility was as perfect as His obedience, so that no thought of His own reputation, or question as to the rightness of the path entered His thoughts. It was the will of God, and in that He delighted.

At Philippi the wild vine of the flesh was beginning to produce its bitter fruits of pride and division. These had not developed as much as in some of the churches to which Paul wrote; but death was working there, and his keen eye detected it, and to arrest the growth of these pernicious things and antidote their deadly effects he brought Christ before them in this way. The meal was cast into the pot.

This is the great remedy. By this is discovered the hatefulness of every carnal work. All fleshly pride stands rebuked in the presence of that lowly life so meekly lived, and if this mind that was in Christ Jesus be in us, we shall walk in grace toward each other and in obedience to God; we shall with lowliness of mind esteem each other more excellent than ourselves, and in humility and obedience work out our own salvation. What place could strife and envy have amongst the saints of God if this mind were in us? Yet this is only possible as the meal is cast into the pot. As we feed upon this life-sustaining food,

"We wonder at Thy lowly mind,
And fain would like Thee be;

*And all our rest and pleasure find
In learning, Lord, of Thee."*

Evil cannot be ignored where it appears, and the works of the flesh must not go unjudged. But no true judgment can be arrived at save in the presence of the perfection of Christ and His Cross. There evil does not appear less evil, but we see it, not only as it spoils our own spiritual good, but how it appears before God; then how great is the relief to turn from it to Christ.

The Holy Spirit is ever ready to fill our thoughts with Christ, and since He is true food for every saint, we find practical unity and fellowship as we feed upon Him. And not only fellowship with each other, but with God also, for He is the Bread of God. "And there was no harm in the pot."

Now mark the next "link" in the chain: *"There came a man from Baal-shalisha, and brought the man of God bread of the first fruits, twenty loaves of barley, and full ears of corn in the husks thereof."* It is deeply interesting that this incident should follow the elimination of the poison and death from the great pot, and it is as instructive as it is interesting. The first fruits were God's portion, but a backslidden Israel forgot His claim and flouted His law (Leviticus 23). This was indeed the chief cause of the dearth in the land. But the man of Baal-shalisha did not forget it, as his present to the man of God proved. The offering of the first fruits of the earth which God claimed spoke typically of that which is of unspeakable value in His account, "the sacrifice of praise, that is, the fruit of our lips, giving thanks to His Name" (Hebrews 13:15). But these spiritual sacrifices will be surely lacking where the life is poisoned by the evil things of the flesh—by the wild gourds, of which I have spoken. If any saint of God, or any company of saints, is to render to God these precious spiritual sacrifices, the flesh must give way to the meekness and gentleness of Christ. It is only when all bitterness, wrath, anger, clamour and evil speaking are put away, and bowels of mercies, kindness, humbleness of mind, meekness, longsuffering, forbearance and forgiveness take their place that the Lord gets His place and portion. It is then that we are free to consider Him, and the Holy Spirit is free to fill us with worship and adoration to Him. Then filled with the Spirit, we can speak to ourselves in psalms, hymns and spiritual songs, singing and making melody in our hearts to the Lord: giving thanks always for all things unto God and the Father in the Name of our Lord Jesus Christ (Ephesians 5:18- 20).

But there is yet another link in this chain which shows us the heart of our Lord. *"And Elisha said, Give unto the people, that they may eat. And his servitor said, What, shall I set this before a hundred men? He said again, Give the people that they may eat: for thus saith the Lord, They shall eat, and shall leave thereof. So he set it before them, and they did eat, and left thereof, according to the Word of the Lord."* Whatever we bring to the Lord in the way of worship and praise He gives back to us in richest blessing, which abounds unto many. If we give to Him what is surely His due—the overflow of glad and worshipping hearts, our souls will be most surely fed and nourished, our very praise which honours Him will edify us. It must be so, even as the men who sat before Elisha were fed with the first fruits that had been presented to him. The servitor did not think much of these first fruits, they would make a poor meal, he thought, for a crowd of hungry men. And it is a common thing, alas, to think little of what is due to the Lord. The popular thought is that the people must be catered for, they must be attracted, and so music and eloquence and ornate services are the order of the day, and that which the Lord prizes is of very little account. "Organised Christianity" is chiefly occupied in pleasing the people, instead of keeping the Lord's Word and not denying His Name, and the Holy Spirit is quenched and grieved and God's household is not fed with meat in due season.

But where the rights of Christ are considered, and He is loved and honoured and adored, the Object of the hearts of His saints and the theme of their praise, the soul-hunger of His people will be met. This shall be, though unspiritual and carnal minded men despise these things that are precious to Christ. He multiplies the provision; His people eat and have enough and to spare. Their souls are fed, and out of full hearts they are able to carry something to others, as did those happy early disciples who went everywhere preaching the Gospel.

"Go and Wash"

*HOW A SIN-STRICKEN SINNER MAY
FIND HEALING AND PEACE*

"Now Naaman, the captain of the host of the king of Syria, was a great man with his master, and honourable, because by him the LORD had given deliverance unto Syria; he was also a mighty man in valour, but he was a leper. And the Syrians had gone out by companies, and had brought away captive out of the land of Israel a little maid; and she waited on Naaman's wife. And she said unto her mistress, Would God my lord were with the prophet that is in Samaria; for he would recover him of his leprosy. And one went in, and told his lord, saying, thus and thus saith the maid that is of the land of Israel. And the king of Syria said, Go to, go, and I will send a letter unto the king of Israel. And he departed, and took with him ten talents of silver, and six thousand pieces of gold, and ten changes of raiment. And he brought the letter to the king of Israel, saying, Now, when this letter is come unto thee, behold, I have therewith sent Naaman my servant to thee, that thou mayest recover him of his leprosy. And it came to pass, when the king of Israel had read the letter, that he rent his clothes, and said, Am I God, to kill and to make alive, that this man doth send unto me to recover a man of his leprosy? Wherefore consider, I pray you, and see how he seeketh a quarrel against me.

And it was so, when Elisha, the man of God, had heard that the king of Israel had rent his clothes, that he sent to the king, saying, Wherefore hast thou rent thy clothes? let him come now to me, and he shall know that there is a prophet in Israel. So Naaman came with his horses and with his chariot, and stood at the door of the house of Elisha. And Elisha sent a messenger unto him, saying, Go and wash in Jordan seven times, and thy flesh shall come again to thee, and thou shalt be clean. But Naaman was wroth, and went away, and said, Behold, I thought, He will surely come out to me, and stand, and call on the Name of the LORD his God, and strike his hand over the place, and recover the leper. Are not Abana and Pharpar, rivers of Damascus, better than all the waters of Israel? may I not wash in them, and be clean? So he turned and went away in a rage. And his servants came near, and spake unto him, and said, My father, if the prophet had bid thee do some great thing, wouldest thou not have done it? how much rather then, when he saith to thee, Wash and be clean? Then went he down, and dipped himself seven times in Jordan, according to the saying of the man of God; and his flesh came again like unto the flesh of a little child, and he was clean."

2 KINGS 5:1-14

Chapter 11
"Go and Wash"

A leper is not a pleasant person to meet. He is an offence both to the eyes and the nostrils, and Naaman was a leper. In many respects he was a great man. He was a successful soldier, and a wise administrator, and Syria had risen to a foremost place among the nations under his leadership. He was valued and honoured by the king, and popular with the people, but he was a leper. He may have done his best to hide the tragic fact from the multitude, but the king knew of it, his own household knew of it, it was talked about by the servants, and what a man's servants talk about the man in the street surely knows, and he knew of it himself. What pleasure could he find in his medals and decorations, his honours, renown, and wealth, or the admiration and the envy of others, when this foul thing was sapping his life and hurrying him on to a loathsome death?

God uses the dreaded disease as a figure of sin in His Word—of SIN. He wants us all to understand how obnoxious sin is to Him, and how corrupting and menacing it is to us and our fellows, and He would teach us by this foul and incurable disease. We speak of this man or that woman being a moral leper. We mean that their lives are gross and offensive, and they are people to be shunned, but every unrepentant, unwashed sinner is a moral leper, let him hide it or camouflage it as he may. Every life that has not God as its centre and object is a sinful life, a leprous life; it is corrupt in its source and outflow, and those who know themselves the best are the readiest to admit it.

A celebrated American writer was offered £10,000 for his autobiography. He replied (I give his exact words): "A man cannot tell the whole truth about himself, even if convinced that what he writes will never be seen by others. I have personally satisfied myself of that, and have got others to test it also. You cannot make bare your private soul and look at it, you are too ashamed, it is too disgusting. For that reason I confine myself to drawing the portraits of others."

Have you felt like that? It may be so, and you have been trying to improve your condition and life, honestly, sincerely; but it has been in vain, the foul water has broken out from the corrupted spring within you when you least wanted or expected it, and your life is a record of broken resolutions and frustrated hopes. What will you do? It is worse than useless to hide the truth from yourself, that would be self-deception, and you cannot deceive others, for they know you by what they know of themselves, or they think they do; least of all can you deceive God. Keep not silent as to this matter before Him, tell your inward grief to God, lay bare your soul before Him, even though the very thought of its corruption disgusts you. David, the great king, said: "When I kept silence, my bones waxed old, through my roaring all the day long; my moisture was turned into the drought of summer." But he saw how foolish he was in that, and he did the right thing at last, for he added: "I acknowledged my transgression, and Thou forgavest the iniquity of my sin" (Psalm 32:3-5). Happy David!

Yes, Naaman was a leper. Fix your eye upon him, for in this respect he is a figure of you as you now appear before God, and it may be that in his story you may learn the way of cleansing and healing.

In Naaman's household there was a little captive maid. Torn from her home by the ruthless Syrians, she shone as a light in her strange and heathen surroundings. Not hatred but compassion filled her young soul, and she was intelligent, too. She knew of the power of the man of God, the prophet in Israel, and so confident of this was she that she bore testimony to it unwaveringly. She knew also the great need in her master's life, and she yearned to bring these two together—the prophet with his power and grace, and the leper with his corruption and misery. Hear her words: "Would God my master were with the prophet that is in Samaria, he would recover him of his leprosy." She was a great evangelist, for of a truth the evangelist needs only to know these two things that she knew—and to know them with conviction and with soul-yearning that others should know them too—the need and the Man Who can meet it.

About a century ago there lived an Irish gentleman named Gideon Ouseley, who was greatly used of God in the blessing of many in his native Ireland, and this was his equipment for the work. In a dream one night he thought he heard the Lord say to him, "Gideon, I want you to preach the Gospel"; and he answered, "Lord, I cannot preach." But the Lord replied, "You know what is wrong with men." "Yes, Lord, I know that", he answered; "they are sinners as I was." "And you know the remedy, don't you?" "Oh, yes, blessed be Thy Name, *I* know the remedy; it is Thyself and Thy Blood." Then said the Lord, "You know the disease and the remedy. Go and tell them of both."

This little maid must have been as consistent as she was compassionate and confident, for her word was believed, and what she said reached the ears of the king, and he, like his great servant, was a man of decision. There was no time to be lost. Naaman must go at once, with all the pomp and parade that befitted his fame, and with a fee large enough to satisfy the most grasping of healers. Naaman was a great man, and Syria was a great country, and now was the time to impress this upon their poor and despised Israelitish neighbours. When Naaman moved out of Damascus with his imposing retinue, most of the people, dazzled by the splendour of it all, would forget the chief fact of all, that Naaman was a leper, and probably that is how he wished it to be. How pride makes men push their sinfulness into the background and parade their wealth and works, their goodness and their charity, their amiability and their religion, the high place they hold in the estimation of their friends or the higher place that they hold in their own. None of these things really count in this supreme question, the great outstanding fact for every unregenerate man is that he is a sinner, as Naaman was a leper. Splendid externals cannot alter that fact.

> *"And facts are chiels that winna ding,*
> *And daurna be disputed."*

And this is the most obstinate, unbeatable, and least to be disputed fact of all: You are a sinner!

We pass over the folly of the king in sending the leper to the wrong person. He only did what thousands are doing to-day. His folly was that of inattention and ignorance, and perhaps pride. He had not given sufficient heed to the words of the little maid, and this was inexcusable in such a grave matter. Yet it is a common fault. We preach Christ and Him crucified as the one Hope of sinners. We tell them plainly, and the Word of God is our authority, that there is no salvation in any other, that none other Name is given under Heaven whereby they must be saved, and they appear to agree with us, and yet go off to other ways and seek through other names the blessing they need. The prophet was little known and perhaps less respected in those days, and the Name of Jesus is not honoured to-day. He is still despised and rejected of men. They think they can do without Him, and win their way to salvation by other means. This is the popular way, alas! the way that seems right to men; but the end thereof are the ways of death (Proverbs 14:12; 16:25). But the king's mistake served to bring into striking evidence the only hope for lepers. "Am I God, to kill and to make alive?" cried the king of Israel, when he read the letter from the king of Syria. But he ought to have known the way, he ought to have been able to instruct this heathen soldier in the way of truth. It was a shame to the king of the land that he knew less than the little captive maid. "Wherefore hast thou rent thy clothes?" said Elisha; "LET HIM COME NOW TO ME, and he shall know that there is a prophet in Israel." Enemy of God's land and people though he has been, pagan though he is, let the poor dying leper come to me, and he shall know! How forcibly we are reminded of the words of our Lord. "Come unto Me, all ye that labour, and are heavy laden, and I will give you rest."

So Naaman came with his horses and his chariot, and stood at the door of the house of Elisha. What a sensation his coming must have caused in that neighbourhood, but

Elisha was not elated. He may have thought that the prophet would have felt highly honoured to have such a visitor at his door, and he certainly expected a great deal of ceremony, but he had to learn that his thoughts were all wrong, and that it was only as a leper that Elisha would deal with him. He would have nothing to say to the great soldier, his honours were of no account in his eyes; but if he would stand forth stripped of all his trappings, a leper, dependent entirely upon the grace and mercy of God, then he would heal him and bless him. It was a hard lesson for a proud man to learn, almost too hard a lesson for Naaman. He resented the prophet's message. "Go and wash in Jordan seven times." In his own land there were nobler rivers, according to his estimation of things, than all the waters of Israel, if to wash was the way of cleansing, he would wash in them and be clean. He was enraged. Up to that day he had always been treated as a great man, and never as a leper. It was unbearable; the insult should be avenged. So he turned away to go back to his own land, with his pride, his gold and silver and raiment and his leprosy.

But God seems to give an angry man another chance. It was so with Cain, and in the case of the elder brother in the story of the prodigal. Here the servants of Naaman, who surely loved their master, pleaded with him with rare tact, and prevailed. Naaman, a humbler and a wiser man, *obeyed* the word of the prophet, and went down into Jordan seven times, and his flesh became as the flesh of a child. He was cleansed and healed.

Now, where do you stand? I address myself to those who have sincerely hoped that their "works of righteousness" would cover their leprosy, who have thought that they could cover their soul-sickness by their endeavours and religion, or who have thought that because the disease of their souls is not so manifest as in some others, they would pass muster at last. Where do you now stand? You do not deny that you are a sinner, but does the word, "Go and wash", offend you? Be assured, there is no other way. If God had bid you do some great thing you would have done it. But nothing you can do can heal your soul or cleanse your sin. "Go and wash" is the word and the way. It is the way for all, and no matter how much a man may resent it in his pride, God can make no exception in His case, for there is no difference in His sight, all have sinned. But where can a sinner wash and be clean? Jordan, as we have already learnt, figures for us death. And it is only through death—Christ's death—that any can have healing and cleansing. Have you not read those great words: "By His stripes we are healed" (Isaiah 53:5), and those others in the New Testament: "The Blood of Jesus Christ, God's Son, cleanseth from all sin" (1 John 1:7)?

"Go in Peace"

HOW THE HEALED ONE FINDS ASSURANCE

"And he returned to the man of God, he and all his company, and came, and stood before him: and he said, Behold, now I know that there is no God in all the earth but in Israel; now therefore, I pray thee, take a blessing of thy servant. But he said, As the LORD liveth, before whom I stand, I will receive none. And he urged him to take it, but he refused. And Naaman said, Shall there not then, I pray thee, be given to thy servant two mules' burden of earth? for thy servant will henceforth offer neither burnt offering not sacrifice unto other gods, but unto the LORD. In this thing the LORD pardon thy servant, that when my master goeth into the house of Rimmon to worship there, and he leaneth on my hand, and I bow down myself in the house of Rimmon: when I bow down myself in the house of Rimmon, the LORD pardon thy servant in this thing. And he said unto him, Go in peace. So he departed from him a little way."

2 KINGS 5:15-19

Chapter 12
"Go in Peace"

THE leper was cleansed, and he returned to God's prophet a humbled and grateful man. There is nothing humbles a man like grace, for grace simply means, what God is for us in Christ, and not what we are for Him; it is what He can do for us, and not what we can do for Him, and it was this lesson that the thankful Syrian had now to learn. He had abandoned his own false thoughts, and he spoke as a man speaks out of whose mind all doubts had been cast. *"Behold, now I know* that there is no God in all the earth but in Israel." The word *"know"* is a great and triumphant word in the Christian's vocabulary, and he has a right to use it, for God Himself puts it into his mouth. When the light of the Gospel breaks into a man's heart, all agnosticism and doubts are driven out, and a full assurance takes possession of it that finds its expression in an unwavering confidence in God and the Word of His grace. Looking upon the past, he can say, "One thing I know, that whereas I was blind, now I see." Thinking of the present, he can read with rejoicing, "These things have I written unto you that believe on the Name of the Son of God; that ye may know that ye have eternal life" (1 John 5:13). And if thoughts arise in the mind as to those sins that stained his soul, he can get assurance as to that matter from the same infallible Word: "Ye know that He was manifested to take away our sins; and in Him was no sin" (1 John 3:5). And again, "I write unto you, little children, because your sins are forgiven you for His Name's sake" (1 John 2:12). And as to the future, what triumphant confidence rings in the words: "We know that if our earthly house of this tabernacle were dissolved, we have a building of God, an house not made with hands, eternal in the heavens" (2 Corinthians 5:1); and, more glorious even than that, "We know that when He shall appear, we shall be like Him, for we shall see Him as He is" (1 John 3:2).

How different is this Christian language to the wail of the agnostic as he gropes his darkened way to the grave. He says:

> *"Is there beyond the silent night a day?*
> *Is death a door that leads to light?*
> *We cannot say.*
> *The tongueless secret locked in fate,*
> *We do not know,*
> *We hope and wait."*

And this confidence is not presumption, any more than was Naaman's. He had proved in his own happy experience what the God of Israel could do for a hopeless leper who would obey Him, and every man who has believed the Gospel of God's salvation, the Good News concerning His Son Jesus Christ our Lord, knows the delivering, peace-giving power of God, and can speak with confidence about it. Yet this confidence does not rest in his experience, blessed as that may have been, but upon the Word of the living God, Who cannot lie. We thank God for the Holy Bible, His sure and unchanging Word. It is there that the Christian finds reliable authority on which to base his confidence. And all the blessing that he enjoys and the peace of true Christian knowledge lie in great facts that other statements of that same Word reveal to us. "We know that the Son of God is come" (1 John 5:20). "We have known and believed the love that God hath to us: GOD IS LOVE" (1 John 4:16). The blessing that Naaman got through Elisha revealed to him the true God, the blessing that we have received through Jesus our Saviour has revealed to us that God is love. "For herein is love, not that we loved God, but that He loved us, and sent His Son to be the propitiation for our sins" (1 John 4:10).

It was natural that Naaman should wish to recompense his benefactor, for, being what he was, he could not understand receiving a great blessing, without money and without price. He felt that he was able to pay for it, and he would do so handsomely. He had to learn that God would not sell His blessing. He was convinced as to the power of God. He had now to learn what His grace was. How emphatic were the words of Elisha: "As the LORD liveth, before Whom I stand, I will receive none." This is a hard lesson for a proud man to learn. "How hardly shall they that have riches enter into the Kingdom of God" (Mark 10:23); whether those riches be in money, or fame, or self-righteousness. Are these of no value? asks their possessor. Well, Naaman possessed an abundance of these sorts of wealth, but they did not and could not cure his leprosy. And it is certain that they cannot atone for a sinner's sins, they cannot save his soul. I am sure that Naaman learnt the great lesson as he stood before Elisha, that God will not sell His blessing, and for two reasons: Naaman, with all his wealth, was too poor to buy it, and God was too rich to sell it. It was all of grace, the free giving of God to one who could not merit His gift. There is no more needed lesson than that for any man to learn.

But let no one suppose that this grace that pardons the sinner and justifies him from all things means that sin is a small thing, and that God can pass over it lightly. No, He cannot do that, and here I quote some invaluable words. "Grace supposes sin to be so horribly bad that God cannot tolerate it. Were it in the power of man, after being unrighteous and evil, to patch up his ways and mend himself so as to stand before God, there would be no need of grace. The very fact of the Lord being gracious shows sin to be so evil a thing, that man, being a sinner, his state is utterly ruined and hopeless, and that nothing but free grace will do for him—it only can meet his need. ... The moment I understand that I am a sinful man, and yet that it was because the Lord knew the full extent of my sin, and what its hatefulness was, that He came to me, I understand what grace is. Faith makes me see that God is greater than my sin, and not that my sin is greater than God" (J. N. Darby). Grace is God's intervention in love on behalf of those who had no power to save themselves, and who were His enemies.

I have no doubt that that great soldier, whose leprous flesh had become like that of a little child, now bowed in a childlike spirit before the man of God, realising that the benefit he had received was beyond all price, and yet that it claimed him henceforward. He most surely belonged to the God Who had given him this new life, and this he must own in the dark land to which he had to return. And so he asks, "Shall there not then, I pray thee, be given to thy servant two mules' burden of earth? For thy servant will henceforth offer neither burnt offering nor sacrifice unto other gods, but unto the Lord." He would raise his altar to God, and confess His Name and worship Him alone. Nothing other than that could be right, and Naaman's vow indicates where lies the Christian's true life and privilege. He has a sacrifice to offer, not for his salvation—for by the offering of Jesus Christ once for all he has been perfected for ever, as Hebrews 10 tells us, and because of that perfect offering his sins and iniquities are to be remembered no more—but because he is saved and belongs to his Saviour. Clear and blessed are the words of Romans 12: "I beseech, therefore, brethren, by the mercies of God, that ye present your bodies a living sacrifice, holy, acceptable to God, which is your reasonable service"; and the one who is saved by grace and knows it will answer such an appeal with a glad response.

Yet Naaman had a fear as he looked into the future. He would be expected to conform to the practices of his idolatrous king and country. "In this thing", he pleaded, "the Lord pardon His servant." The prophet's answer was a very brief one. "Go in peace", was all that he had to say. Did this mean that a confessor of the true God could compromise with idolatry, and be conformed to the world? Surely not. It means, Leave that with God. The God Who has healed you can keep you. Leave your future in His hands, go in peace. "For God is faithful, Who will not suffer you to be tempted above that ye are able; but will with the temptation also make a way of escape, that ye may be able to bear it" (1 Corinthians 10:13). It may be that there is one among my readers who is trembling on the very threshold of the Christian life, feeling that a whole-hearted yielding of his life is the only right answer to the grace so rich and free that has saved him, yet fearing the consequences, and most of all his own weakness in circumstances that seem too difficult for him. Here are great words and comforting for him: "Be careful for nothing; but in everything by prayer and supplication with thanksgiving let your requests be made known unto God. And the peace of God which passeth all understanding shall keep your hearts and minds through Christ Jesus" (Philippians 4:6, 7). With words like these in the heart, the saved and happy, trusting soul may "Go in peace".

The Axe-Head did Swim

*HOW THOSE WHO ARE DEAD MAY
HAVE ETERNAL LIFE*

"And the sons of the prophets said unto Elisha, Behold, now, the place where we dwell with thee is too strait for us. Let us go, we pray thee, unto Jordan, and take thence every man a beam, and let us make a place there, where we may dwell, And he answered, Go ye. And one said, Be content, I pray thee, and go with thy servants. And he answered, I will go. So he went with them. And when they came to Jordan, they cut down wood. But as one was felling a beam, the axe-head fell into the water, and he cried, and said, Alas! master! for it was borrowed. And the man of God said, Where fell it? And he shewed him the place. And he cut down a stick, and cast it in thither; and the iron did swim. Therefore said he, Take it up to thee. And he put out his hand and took it."

2 KINGS 6:1-7

Chapter 13
The Axe-Head did Swim

WHAT highly favoured men these sons of the prophets were in being the companions and disciples of Elisha. His words must have been good to listen to, and it is no wonder that they crowded to hear him until the place where they dwelt with him could not contain them, and they felt that they needed more room. It was a healthy sign, and their desire for enlargement had the full approval of the prophet.

Are we dwelling with our Lord as those sons of the prophets dwelt with Elisha? "I will never leave thee nor forsake thee", He has said, and He will not deny His own Word. But are we consciously dwelling with Him? We often quote His words: "Where two or three are gathered together in My Name, there am I in the midst of them"; but are they mere words to us, or a living reality? If we are dwelling with the Lord and learning of Him, we are growing; we are being enlarged in our souls, and we shall want to move on in the more abundant life that is ours.

This question of growth is a vital one. A father would be seriously concerned if his children ceased to develop in mind and body, and God is our Father—does He not care whether His children are growing in grace or not? He certainly does. Let us not be indifferent to this matter, for growth and strength go together, and we cannot be strong in the face of the foe if we do not grow and move on in the knowledge of the Lord; we shall not be more than conquerors if we stagnate and are stunted in growth. To the Church at Corinth Paul wrote: "O ye Corinthians, our mouth is opened unto you, our heart is enlarged. Ye are not straitened in us, but ye are straitened in your own bowels. Now for a recompense in the same (I speak as unto my children), BE YE ALSO ENLARGED" (2 Corinthians 6:11-13).

What was it that had straitened and stunted those Christians? The world and the evil things that are in it. They had forgotten that the Gospel of their salvation had called them out of the world to brighter and better things, and that they had been united to Christ, Who is not of the world, by the Holy Ghost from Heaven. They had formed associations which made it impossible for them to expand in the greatness of the Christian life and service—they were fettered and not free, and they needed the command, "Be ye not unequally yoked with unbelievers. … Come out from among them and be ye separate, saith the Lord, And touch not the unclean thing" (2 Corinthians 6:14, 17). We cannot love and cleave to the world and abide in Christ at the same time. To dwell as His disciples with Him means separation from the world, and there can be no spiritual growth apart from this.

It was to JORDAN that these young men went for the material with which to build their larger dwelling, and there is no place like Jordan for enlargement of soul, for Jordan is a figure of death. Death is a great and effectual teacher; it teaches how great is the fall of man, for death is the measure of it, and it teaches us how great is the love of God, for "He commendeth His love toward us, in that while we were yet sinners, *Christ died for us*" (Romans 5:8). Death shows us the way that God has taken to recover His fallen creature for Himself, and to bring him into larger blessing than was possible for him before he fell.

The incident of the loss and recovery of the borrowed axe-head shall illustrate these things for us. I do not think that I am giving it a fanciful interpretation in so using it; if my readers think so, let them forget the illustration and consider the truth that I am pressing. The axe-head fell from the handle of it, and sank beneath the waters of Jordan. The wielder of it was a careless man, for the axe was borrowed, it was not his to lose, but it was lost nevertheless. Thus carelessly did Adam become a lost soul; and it was to God that he was lost, as is clearly proved by God's cry in the Garden, "Adam, where art thou?"

By that one act of disobedience death entered into the world. So we read in Romans 5:12: "By one man sin entered into the world, and death by sin; AND SO DEATH PASSED UPON ALL MEN: FOR THAT ALL HAVE SINNED." Yes, the waters of Jordan roll over the whole race of sinners as a result of the first man's disobedience, a disobedience in which all his progeny have shared, for they have all been as wilful as he. Adam had no right to cast away his soul, for it belonged to God Who had created it and given it to him. When he fell, the whole race of which he was the progenitor fell with him. All Scripture as well as all history teaches this solemn truth, but nowhere is it stated more emphatically than in the fifth chapter of Romans. Verse 15 says: "Through the offence of one many be dead"; verse 17: "By one man's offence death reigned by one"; verse 18: "By the offence of one, judgment came upon all men to condemnation"; verse 19: "By one man's disobedience many were made sinners."

That is not a popular doctrine. The foolish theory of Evolution suits the modern mind better than the solemn truth. Men want to get rid of the thought that they are responsible to God and must give account to Him. And this is why the fact of the Fall is refused; and this is why the fiction of Evolution is embraced; it is more pleasant to believe that man is rising up, becoming greater and grander as the ages pass by, than to own that he is sinful, fallen and lost. But the latter is the truth. Just as the nature of the axe-head was to sink and not swim, to go down, with no power in itself to rise up, so man's nature as a sinful, fallen creature is to go farther and farther from God; his course is ever downward, as is plainly shown to us in Romans 1:19-32, which solemn Scripture my readers should seriously ponder. Nothing but the truth will satisfy a fully awakened conscience, and the truth is clearly stated in these Scriptures that I have quoted. Blessed is the man who will own it before God.

This son of a prophet was conscious of his loss, and he felt it the more because the axe was borrowed; but he was wise in that he did not waste his time in vain efforts to recover what he had lost, but cried to the man of God, "Alas, master!" And here is a fine example for sinful men. The first step to recovery and blessing is to realise the need and the loss, but some who have taken this step are seeking sincerely and earnestly to right what is wrong by their own efforts. They are endeavouring by their works to save themselves, when the Scripture states expressly "Not of works, lest any man should boast" (Ephesians 2:9).

The man of God was equal to the situation. And in this he did faintly foreshadow the all-sufficiency of Christ,

Who came into the world to destroy the power of death and set us free. "Where fell it?" asked the man of God. Then cutting down a branch of a tree, he cast it into the water, and lo! the iron did swim! Do you perceive in this incident the Gospel story? And does that story thrill your soul? How wonderful it is! It tells of Jesus, Who went into death for us that we might pass out of death into life. Yet the question might well arise, "If death has passed upon all men, if all are dead in trespasses and sins, so that none can deliver either himself or his brother, what was there in Jesus that made Him different to others? Who was He?" He was the only begotten Son of God, He was the Word, the Creator of all things, and He became flesh and dwelt among us. He became flesh—a man, as truly man as Adam was, or as any man is to-day—but the SINLESS MAN, and in this He differed from all others. In becoming man He did not cease to be the only-begotten, eternal Son of God. This great truth we must hold fast in the face of modern infidelity. He Who was in the form of God was found in the likeness of men. He had become a man that He might die for men. Yet as a man death had no claim upon Him, for He was holy. Yes, He was just as holy as He trod the dusty roads of Galilee as when He sat upon the Throne of His glory and created the hosts of Heaven. Because He was holy, the one sinless Man, death had no claim upon Him. He could have walked victoriously upon death's fiercest billows, just as He trod upon the waves of the Sea of Galilee at midnight. But He came to die. This commandment He had received from His Father, and just as the branch of the tree—the nature of which was to swim—was cast into the waters by Elisha, that the iron—the nature of which was to sink—might swim, so Jesus, upon Whom death had no claim, went down into death that we, whom death held in its power, might pass out of death into life, that we might live in Him Who died for us and rose again.

This is God's way of salvation, the way that His great love has found, and as we consider it we are greatly enlarged; we are delivered from bondage and set free by the truth, for the truth is that "GOD IS LOVE", and "in this was manifested the love of God toward us, because that God sent His only begotten Son into the world, that we might live through Him" (1 John 4:9).

"Take it up to thee", said the prophet, and he put out his hand and took it, a grateful and wondering man, as well he might be. I desire that we might understand better those words of the Lord: "Verily, verily, I say unto you, he that heareth My word, and believeth on Him that sent Me, hath everlasting life, and shall not come into con-demnation, but is passed from death unto life" (John 5:24). If we have heard the words of this glorious Gospel, which first began to be spoken by our Lord, and have believed on God the Father Who sent Him to tell them to us, this eternal life is ours; we have put forth the hand of faith and taken it; our souls are saved, we are recovered from death, and now we live. But how shall we live, and to whom? There is only one right answer, and it is a Scriptural one: "The love of Christ constraineth us; because we thus judge, that if One died for all, then were all dead: and that He died for all, that THEY WHICH LIVE SHOULD NOT HENCEFORTH LIVE UNTO THEMSELVES, BUT UNTO HIM WHICH DIED FOR THEM AND ROSE AGAIN" (2 Corinthians 5:14, 15). We could have no better com-mentary on our Old Testament story than that Scripture, and every redeemed heart and conscience says "That is right." The life that is lived unto Christ is the victorious life; in it we are more than conquerors and in no other. In it our souls will be enlarged in the knowledge of God and of Christ.

"He Saved Himself, not Once nor Twice"

*HOW TO ESCAPE THE SNARES
OF THE DEVIL*

"Then the king of Syria warred against Israel, and took counsel with his servants, saying, In such and such a place shall be my camp. And the man of God sent unto the king of Israel, saying, Beware that thou pass not such a place; for thither the Syrians are come down. And the king of Israel sent to the place which the man of God told him, and warned him of, and saved himself there, not once nor twice. Therefore the heart of the king of Syria was sore troubled for this thing; and he called his servants, and said unto them, Will ye not show me which of us is for the king of Israel? And one of his servants said, None, my lord, O king; but Elisha, the prophet that is in Israel, telleth the king of Israel the words that thou speakest in thy bedchamber."

2 KINGS 6:8-12

Chapter 14
"He Saved Himself, not Once nor Twice"

A master of strategy was this king of Syria, and carefully and well he prepared his plan of campaign. An ambush here, another there, and still a third, and surely the unsuspecting king of Israel would be trapped and his kingdom fall into the hands of his conqueror. But he failed; all his plans went wrong; the king of Israel saved himself, not once nor twice. And this Syrian strategist, so sure of success, was a baffled and puzzled man. He could only account for it in one way: there must be a traitor in his camp, a Judas in his war council. But it wasn't that. He hadn't taken into his consideration the fact that there was a God in Israel and that He was represented there by His prophet. But now the secret comes out, for one of his servants knew it. "Elisha, the prophet that is in Israel, tells the king of Israel the words that thou speakest in thy bedchamber." That was it. All his secrets were known to the prophet, and the king of Israel was in contact with the prophet, and he hearkened to his word and obeyed it, and so he saved himself from the snares of his adversary. In the simple and arresting words of Scripture, "HE SAVED HIM-SELF, NOT ONCE NOR TWICE."

This story was written for our learning, as were all the others in these Old Testament Scriptures, and in spite of our weakness we'll be a wise and happy people if we pay heed to its lesson. The Syrian king is a picture of Satan, and in him we have a subtle foe. "Satan hath desired to have you, that he may sift you as wheat", said the Lord to Simon (Luke 22:31). And he is not dead or decrepit, nor any less malicious or alert now. This great adversary of the saints of God is ever on the outlook to catch them alive, and he lays his snares for them with all the subtlety of that old serpent that ensnared the first woman and man in Eden.

We read in the New Testament of some who had fallen into the snare of the Devil and were taken captive by him at his will. He has made a careful study of every one of us; he knows our propensities and weaknesses, and he lays his snares for us with consummate skill. We must not under-rate our foe; we are no match for him. If we meet him in our own strength and wisdom, we shall be as fools in the hands of a sharper. How, then, can we save ourselves not once nor twice from his traps?

If the king of Syria shows us what Satan and his ways are, Elisha is a figure of our living Lord, our ever watchful and all-wise Saviour. The Devil is neither omnipotent nor omniscient; he does not possess fore-knowledge; these are Divine attributes, and they dwell in our Lord. The Devil never got ahead of our Lord, all his plans for ensnaring our feet and destroying our faith are foreseen and antici-pated. "I have prayed for thee", He said to Simon, and if that self-confident disciple had but heeded the word of his Master he would have saved himself from his foe, and the Devil would have registered a great failure, as indeed he did afterwards, when Simon, having escaped by the grace and prayer of the Lord, in the power of the Holy Ghost, made a mighty onslaught on his kingdom and delivered three thousand souls from his power.

Our safety lies in cleaving to the Lord with purpose of heart; we must keep in continual communication with Him. He watches us even more closely than the Devil does, for His love for us is greater than even the Devil's hatred for us. He cares for us with a constant and enduring love, and this should keep us close to His side.

> *"With foes and snares around us,*
> *And lusts and fears within,*
> *The grace that sought and found us,*
> *Alone can keep us clean."*

If we are close to Him, He will minister His Word to us as we need it, and we shall be able to say: *"By the words of Thy lips I have kept me from the paths of the destroyer. Hold up my goings in Thy paths, that my footsteps slip not"* (Psalm 17:4, 5).

Here is illustrated for us those words that are a puzzle to some: "Work out your own salvation with fear and trembling." This cannot be done apart from obedience to the Word of the Lord. By that Word we are forewarned and forearmed, and the man who gives heed to its teaching will save both himself and those that hear him (1 Timothy 4:16). "Wherewithal shall a young man cleanse his way? by taking heed according to Thy Word" (Psalm 119:9). But the words of Scripture can only be rightly understood and obeyed as we are near to the Lord; it is when we are near to Him that they become indeed His communications to us, we are stimulated by them to spiritual alertness, and Satan does not get an advantage against us, and we are not ignorant of his wiles (2 Corinthians 2:11).

What a thankful man the king of Israel must have been. We do not know how he treated Elisha, but we know how he ought to have treated him. He ought to have said to him, "Be my friend and counsellor at all times, guide me in all my ways, correct me, preserve me from folly, and bless me. Live with me, never leave me nor forsake me, for thou art indispensable to my safety and well-being." Is it thus we address our Lord? Let us hear what He says to us. "If a man love Me, he will keep My words, and My Father will love him, and We will come and make Our abode with him" (John 14:23). And how safe from all the snares of the Devil all such must be.

> *"How blest are they who still abide,*
> *Close sheltered by His watchful side;*
> *Who life and strength from Him receive,*
> *And with Him move, and in Him live."*

"Horses and Chariots of Fire"

HOW TO BE WITHOUT FEAR OF
OUR FOES

"And he said, Go and spy where he is, that I may send and fetch him. And it was told him, saying, Behold, he is in Dothan. Therefore sent he thither horses and chariots, and a great host: and they came by night, and compassed the city about. And when the servant of the man of God was risen early and gone forth, behold, an host compassed the city both with horses and chariots. And his servant said unto him, Alas, my master! how shall we do? And he answered, Fear not: for they that be with us are more than they that be with them. And Elisha prayed and said, LORD, I pray Thee, open his eyes that he may see. And the LORD opened the eyes of the young man; and he saw: and, behold, the mountain was full of horses and chariots of fire round about Elisha."

2 KINGS 6:13-17

Chapter 15
"Horses and Chariots of Fire"

If the Devil cannot ensnare you with his wiles, he will change his tactics, he will stop his beguiling, and begin to buffet you; he will show himself to be your implacable adversary, for his name "Satan" means "the adversary". John Bunyan, who knew his ways if ever a man did, tells us in thrilling words of his effort to scare the Pilgrim to the Celestial City from his purpose. He says: "He straddled quite across the whole breadth of the way", and said to Christian, "I sware by my infernal den that thou shalt go no farther: here will I spill thy blood."

That is his way. He will do his desperate worst to make you feel that a life of faith is beset with dangers and insurmountable difficulties, in the hope of shaking your faith in God. This is plainly illustrated in our story.

The city where Elisha lodged was surrounded in the night by a great force of Syrian warriors, and when the servant of the man of God awoke he was filled with fear. The foe was entrenched at every gate, there was no way of escape, and he began to feel that for all his trust in Elisha he was on the losing side. He was wise in running to his master, but his cry, "Alas, my master, how shall we do?" plainly showed how shaken he was by the sight of the enemy's power.

Have you ever felt like that? It may be that even now some of my readers are finding that their confession of Christ has brought them up against difficulties that they never anticipated, and with which they feel utterly unable to cope. Are you surprised? "In the world ye shall have tribulation", and if that were all you might well consider whether you were wise in standing against the force of the foe for Christ's sake, but Jesus added to those words: "But be of good cheer, I have overcome the world" (John 16:33). And the way of escape is not in lowering the standard and compromising with the foe, and being less of a Christian in the hope of some relief, but in turning afresh to the Lord, even if it is with the almost despairing cry of Elisha's servant. He is the great Overcomer. He died, but He lives again, and He ever liveth to make intercession for you, and herein lies the way of confidence and victory for you. Let us consider it.

First notice that Elisha prayed for his terrified servant, and his intercession prevailed to quieten his fears. Your great Intercessor prays for you, and He is never deceived by the Devil; let him scheme and rage as he will, your Lord is always ahead of him, and He ever liveth to make intercession for you. And here is a theme that might well occupy volumes printed in gold, but how little understood! If you have not considered it, do so now; deliverance from all fear of the enemy depends entirely upon the grace and mercy that you may receive through the intercession of our Lord and Saviour Jesus Christ. He is our Great High Priest, the Son of God. Does not your heart swell with holy exultation at the thought of His greatness? The service to which He devotes Himself in this character is that of bearing up His warring pilgrims in intercession before

God, and He does this with truest compassion and deepest sympathy. He is touched with the feeling of our infirmities—marvellous thought!

You may not be able to understand it; you are not asked to do so, it is too great for your small mind; but He asks you to believe it, and if you don't you will grieve that heart that loves above all things to be trusted. He would have you to believe that He is serving you every hour because He loves you; yes, loves you with the same love that led Him to Calvary for you. The birth pangs do not exhaust the mother's love for her babe; she would be willing to lay down her life for it at any time.

> *"Yet she may forgetful prove,*
> *He will never cease to love."*

How could He cease to love? He is Jesus. And what does that Name mean to us? It tells us of the love that brought Him from the Eternal Throne to Bethlehem's manger; it tells us of a life of suffering-service that led through sorrow and shame and loss to the Cross of Calvary; it tells us how His love declared itself there. The waves of death uplifted their awful crests and rolled upon Him to engulf Him; the billows of Satan's power roared about Him to destroy Him, and He went down beneath the deep waters of God's judgment against sin on our behalf. But though He stood for us where all the seas met upon Him, yet was not His love quenched. It burned with a fervent flame amidst the fierce waters, and shed its wondrous light in the darkness of that awful hour, and there it triumphed. Now the Lord is risen: He lives upon the Throne of God for us:

> *"And we stand beyond the doom*
> *Of all our sins through Jesus' empty tomb."*

His love has not changed one whit; it is as deeply interested in your welfare to-day as it was when it bore your sins on the tree. Were it otherwise, Jesus would no longer bear that precious Name for us, and we should have neither Saviour, Priest, nor Defender.

But Jesus is the Son of God, for so the Word presents Him, and while "Jesus" carries us in thought down to the very depths of the humiliation into which His love carried Him, "THE SON OF GOD" presents His glory, His magnificent greatness, the unmeasured splendour of His Person and inheritance. But there are other thoughts than these in the bringing together of these names and titles that should talk eloquently to our hearts. "Jesus" tells us of His preciousness to us. "The Son of God" tells us of His preciousness to God. "JESUS" TELLS US THAT, SINCE HE LOVES US SO WELL, THERE IS NOTHING THAT WOULD BE GOOD FOR US THAT HE WILL NOT ASK FOR US WHEN HE INTERCEDES BEFORE GOD FOR US; AND "SON OF GOD" TELLS US THAT GOD WILL NOT DENY HIM ANY REQUEST THAT HE MAKES. So that the fact of Jesus, the Son of God, being our Great High Priest, means that we are put into contact with the eternal and inexhaustible grace and power of God, and infinite love sets these resources in motion for us, for God loves His Son, and Jesus loves us, and Jesus is the Son of God. Who would fear the Devil who knows the blessedness of this?

Our limited space forbids that we should enlarge upon this most blessed theme, but we would urge upon our readers, and especially those who are passing through trial and sorrow, who are confronted with difficulties and opposition to their faith that make them afraid, to consider the High Priest of our profession, Christ Jesus. He it is Who intercedes for you and Who can and will sustain you. He has passed through the heavens from the very

lowest point of suffering and shame; He has gone to the
highest point in glory, and no watchful sentry rang out
the challenge, "Halt!" for every gate was thrown open
wide for Him to pass triumphantly through, and He is
our Forerunner in the glory as well as our Priest. There is
not a difficulty or hostile power that He has not met in
the way that we travel as we follow Him. He was tempted
in all points as we are, apart from sin. And now He lives
in glory to succour us with gracious help from thence.

But Elisha not only prayed for the young man, he spoke
to him, and what assuring words they were. "Fear not," he
said, "for they that be with us are more than they that be
with them." And the word of Elisha opened his eyes, and
lo! the mountain was full of horses and chariots of fire
round about Elisha. How safe he was in the company of
his master. With his eyes opened he might well have
shouted with triumph, "If God be for us, who can be
against us?" And that is just where we stand through
grace. God is round about us, why should we be afraid?

> "E'en friends may pass and perish, Thou, God, wilt not remove;
> No hatred of the devil can part me from Thy love;
> No hungering, nor thirsting, no poverty nor care,
> No wrath of mighty princes can reach my shelter there.
> No angel and no demon, no throne, nor power, nor might,
> No love, no tribulation, no danger, fear nor fight,
> No height, no depth, no creature that has been or can be,
> Can drive me from Thy bosom, can sever me from Thee."

Let the assuring words of our Saviour sing their sweet
melody to our hearts: "The Father Himself loveth you,
because ye have loved Me"; "Let not your heart be troubled, neither let it be afraid."

God never abandoned a man who stood for Him. "Our
fathers trusted in Thee and were delivered." The Hebrew
youths in the furnace of fire, Daniel in the den of lions,

Elisha and his servant in Dothan, proclaim the fact for us that God stands by those who are true to Him. To us the Lord has said, "I will not leave thee, neither will I forsake thee." So that taking courage we may say, "The Lord is my helper, and I will not be afraid; what will men do unto me?" (Hebrews 13:5, 6). The Devil is just as powerless as men if the Lord is with us.

It is a great day in our spiritual history when we learn that God has bound us up with the interests and fortunes of His dear Son, and that He is not against us but for us. If God were against us, we could not but despair; but He is for us, and if God be for us, who can be against us? That is a great triumphant challenge! "I am thy shield", He said to Abraham. He is ours also, to stand between us and every foe, to answer every charge, and to drive away all fear of the foe from our breast. Having given His Son for us, will He withhold any good? And if He allows us to suffer, to be killed all the day long for Christ's sake, in these things we are more than conquerors through Him that loved us. The enemy may take a Christian's possession from him, and even his life, if God permit it, but he cannot destroy his faith or separate him from the love of God which is in Christ Jesus our Lord. It is in the knowledge that God is for us that we are delivered from all fear in the path of faith, and this knowledge will ever be real to us if we keep in the company of our Lord Jesus Christ.

"Shall I smite them?"

HOW GOOD MAY TRIUMPH
OVER EVIL

"And it came to pass, when they were come into Samaria, that Elisha said, LORD, open the eyes of these men, that they may see. And the LORD opened their eyes, and they saw, and behold, they were in the midst of Samaria. And the king of Israel said unto Elisha when he saw them, My father, shall I smite them? shall I smite them? And he answered, Thou shalt not smite them: wouldest thou smite those whom thou hast taken captive with thy sword and with thy bow? Set bread and water before them, that they may eat and drink and go to their master. And he prepared great provision for them, and when they had eaten and drunk, he sent them away, and they went to their master. So the bands of Syria came no more into the land of Israel."

2 KINGS 6:20-23

Chapter 16
"Shall I smite them?"

The would-be captors were taken captive; for all their show of might they were helpless prisoners when the Lord displayed Himself on the behalf of His servant. If we have been kept and sustained by the great fact that God is for us, and are fearless when foes threaten us, because of this we may well triumph, but now comes the need of special watchfulness. If the wiles and might of the Devil both fail to turn us from the Lord and the life of faith, he will endeavour to incite the flesh within us and make us act in times of testing on our natural impulses. The danger that lies here is illustrated for us in the king of Israel's feelings towards these captive Syrians. They were his enemies; much trouble they had given him, and many sleepless nights and anxious days; they had plotted his overthrow, and would have accomplished their purpose if he had not kept in constant communication with the man of God; and now they were in his power, he could repay them for all the evil they had done him, he could avenge himself of them now, his turn had come. His hand flew to his sword hilt, and he cried to the man of God, with more enthusiasm than he showed in most things: "My father, shall I smite them? Shall I smite them?"

It is not difficult to picture his eagerness, and we can understand it well. This king was very human, so very like ourselves; we feel that our impulse would have been just what his was if we had been in his place. Indeed, I have no doubt that a feeling of shame begins to rise within our hearts as we see ourselves in this rash king. We have been wronged by some one who ought to have known better, and we made up our minds that when the opportunity came we would smite, we would avenge ourselves. We knew the feeling was wrong, and we lost our joy and peace by nursing it; but there it was, revenge is sweet to the flesh, and revenged we would be. How often the Devil has laughed in his triumph over the children of God when they have cultivated and displayed this spirit.

We have to learn that if God had retaliated upon us because of our sins we should have perished for ever. But He did not. He overcame our evil by His good, and He saved us by His grace. Though we had been His enemies, yet He forgave us for Christ's sake. We are not now in the flesh but in the Spirit (Romans 8), and the fruits of the Spirit and not the works of the flesh are to be manifested in us. The life of Jesus has now to be seen in us; we are to be like Him. His enemies were merciless and implacable; they pursued Him with their bitter hatred throughout His life, and were not satisfied until they had nailed Him to a cross, and what did He do when they had done their worst? He prayed: "Father, forgive them, for they know not what they do" (Luke 23:34).

But it is not easy to forgive. He was so unkind to you, and the things he said were so false, and you were so deeply wounded; and she has been so unreasonable and persistent in her enmity that you feel you cannot forgive! No, you cannot! But you will if you are near enough to the Lord, just as the king of Israel forgave through being near to Elisha. Elisha was the prophet of grace, and this was an opportunity for the display of grace; these Syrians must go back to their master persuaded that there was a temper in Israel that was not known in Syria, and so Elisha said, "Thou shalt not smite them. ... Set bread and water before them, that they may eat and drink, and go to their master." It does not appear to have been hard for the king of Israel to do this. He seems to have caught Elisha's spirit and acted on it with a very good will, for HE PREPARED GREAT PROVISION FOR THEM; and when they had eaten and drunk, he sent them away, and they went to their master. And the king gained a greater victory by his kindness than he could have gained by his prowess upon the battlefield, for the bands of Syrians troubled him no more.

This is the way of victory, to suffer and bear it patiently, to overcome evil with good, to meet enmity with the spirit of grace and forgiveness; this was the Lord's way with His foes, and He has left us an example that we should thus follow in His steps: "Who did no sin, neither was guile found in His mouth: Who when He was reviled, reviled not again: when He suffered He threatened not: but committed Himself to Him that judgeth righteously: Who His own self bare our sins in His own body on the tree, that we, being dead to sins, should live unto righteousness, by Whose stripes we are healed" (1 Peter 2:22-24). And we only live unto righteousness as His own life and grace show themselves in us.

And if this grace must be shown to those that are without, what about our brethren? How often must we forgive them? It was a generous impulse that moved the heart of Peter, when his long association with his Lord made him suggest that he might go the length of forgiving his brother seven times! And what a glow of satisfaction

141

would pervade his soul as he made the suggestion. Surely the Lord would praise him and hold him up as an example of grace to the other disciples.

But what said the Lord? "I say not unto thee. Until seven times: but until seventy times seven" (Matthew 18:22).

We can almost hear Peter's gasp of astonishment, and see his jaw drop. How mean were his ideas of forgiveness and grace really, when brought to the true standard, and yet he was far ahead of many Christians. When Peter got over the shock of these wonderful words, we can understand him saying, "But, Master, that is impossible; human nature could not do it. You are asking too much of me." How patiently, how tenderly, the Lord would reply, "That is the way I am treating you, Peter; I only ask and expect you to treat others as I am treating you." It is the deep soul-knowledge of this unlimited grace of our Lord which we can only know as we are near to Him that will make us ready to fulfil the Lord's words. We shall say, "Lord, we obey Thy Word, we obey it gladly, we can do no other." And we shall find that the joy of forgiving is an unspeakable joy. It is the very joy of God that He permits us to share with Him.

But there is more than this in the great revelation of God's grace and purposes towards us in Christ Jesus. God has forgiven us for Christ's sake, and this is given as the reason why we should be kind to one another, tender-hearted, forgiving one another (Ephesians 4:32). But in the Colossian Epistle an inconceivable grace is unfolded to us. We learn in heart-moving words that we are united to Christ. He is the Head in Heaven, and we, His Blood-bought and Holy Ghost-sealed saints, are His Body on earth. We learn the great fact that the life of the Head in Heaven is in His Body on earth, and that now in the very world where Christ was crucified and where Satan stirred up men to destroy the temple of His body, He has a Body in which His life and the graces of it are being displayed, and forgiveness has a prominent place in this life. Consider the passage which shows this. "Put on, therefore, as the elect of God, holy and beloved, bowels of mercies, kindness, humbleness of mind, meekness, long-suffering, forbearing one another, and *forgiving one another, if any man have a quarrel against any: even as Christ forgave you, so also do ye*" (Colossians 3:12, 13). What a wonderful standard that is. Christ's forgiveness is complete and eternal, for He has made us members of His own Body, but in doing that He has made us members one of another; as we remember that we shall bear no grudge against any Christian. "As Christ forgave you, so also do ye", will be our measure and our way.

Then Satan's efforts to stir up our hearts to anger and wrath and malice against those who do not treat us well will fail, and instead of being overcome by these fleshly feelings, we shall manifest the grace of our Lord and Head, and even in these things be more than conquerors through Him that loved us.

"A Day of Good Tidings"

*HOW THE FAMINE WAS
CHANGED TO A FEAST*

"And it came to pass after this, that Ben-hadad, king of Syria, gathered all his host, and went up and besieged Samaria. And there was a great famine in Samaria: and, behold, they besieged it, until an ass's head was sold for fourscore pieces of silver, and the fourth part of a cab of doves' dung for five pieces of silver. And as the king of Israel was passing by upon the wall, there cried a woman unto him, saying, Help, my lord, O king. And he said, If the LORD do not help thee, whence shall I help thee? out of the barnfloor, or out of the winepress? And the king said unto her, What aileth thee? And she answered, This woman said unto me, Give thy son, that we may eat him to-day, and we will eat my son to-morrow. So we boiled my son, and did eat him; and I said unto her on the next day, Give thy son, that we may eat him; and she hath hid her son. And it came to pass, when the king heard the words of the woman, that he rent his clothes; and he passed by upon the wall, and the people looked, and behold, he had sackcloth within upon his flesh. Then he said, God do so and more also to me, if the head of Elisha, the son of Shaphat, shall stand on him this day. ...

2 KINGS 6:24-31

Then Elisha said, Hear ye the word of the LORD: Thus saith the LORD, To-morrow about this time shall a measure of fine flour be sold for a shekel, and two measures of barley for a shekel, in the gate of Samaria. Then a lord on whose hand the king leaned, answered the man of God, and said, Behold, if the LORD would make windows in Heaven, might this thing be? And he said, Behold, thou shalt see it with thine eyes, but shalt not eat thereof. And there were four leprous men at the entering in of the gate: and they said one to another, Why sit we here until we die? If we say, We will enter into the city, then the famine is in the city, and we shall die there; and if we sit still here, we die also. Now therefore come, and let us fall into the host of the Syrians: if they save us alive we shall live; and if they kill us, we shall but die. And they rose up in the twilight to go unto the camp of the Syrians, and when they were come to the uttermost part of the camp of Syria, behold, there was no man there. For the Lord had made the host of the Syrians to hear a noise of chariots, and a noise of horses, even the noise of a great host: and they said one to another, Lo, the king of Israel hath hired against us the kings of the Hittites, and the kings of the Egyptians, to come upon us. Wherefore they arose and fled in the twilight, and left their tents, and their horses, and their asses, even the camp as it was, and fled for their life. And when these lepers came to the uttermost part of the camp, they went into one tent, and did eat and drink, and carried thence silver and gold and raiment, and went and hid it; and came again, and entered into another tent, and carried thence also, and went and hid it. Then they said one to another, We do not well: this day is a day of good tidings, and we hold our peace; if we tarry till the morning light, some mischief will come upon us: now therefore come, that we may go and tell the king's household. ...

2 Kings 7:1-9

They took therefore two chariot horses, and the king sent after the host of the Syrians, saying, Go and see. And they went after them unto Jordan; and lo, all the way was full of garments and vessels, which the Syrians had cast away in their haste. And the messengers returned and told the king. And the people went out, and spoiled the tents of the Syrians. So a measure of fine flour was sold for a shekel and two measures of barley for a shekel, according to the word of the LORD."

2 KINGS 7:14-16

Chapter 17
"A Day of Good Tidings"

NEVER was there a city in a worse case than this Samaria. The strong foe outside, and the sore famine inside had most surely brought them to the verge of despair. So reduced were they that mothers were boiling and eating their children, and if that seems an incredible thing, my answer is, it was but the fulfilment of the Word of God. These Israelites were great sinners. They had ignored the commandments of their God, and done their own wicked wills, and He had warned them long ago as to what the consequences of such rebellion against Him would be. In Deuteronomy 28 we read: "The tender and delicate woman among you, which would not adventure to set the sole of her foot upon the ground for delicateness and tenderness, her eye shall be evil … toward her young one that cometh out from between her feet, and toward her children which she shall bear; for she shall eat them for want of all things secretly in the siege and straightness wherewith thine enemy shall distress thee in thy gates. If thou wilt not observe to do all the words of this law that are written in this Book" (verses 56-58). Now it had turned out as the Word had predicted, undeniable evidence that the Word of God must be fulfilled. Heaven and earth shall pass away, but not one jot or tittle of His Word can fail, and it will be well with those who take heed to those words. But did this great chastisement change the hearts of the people? No, it did not, for we conclude that they were truly represented by their king, and he, when he heard this gruesome tale, did not cry out to God for mercy. He did not say, "O God, we have sinned against Thee, and Thy judgment is just, but now pardon Thy people and deliver them." No, he swore an oath, saying, "God, do so, and more also, to me, if the head of Elisha, the son of Shaphat, shall stand upon him this day." He set out to murder the only one who could bless them. It was a strange thing, for this surely was the same king who had been delivered in former days by Elisha, yet now his one desire was to murder the man who had been his most faithful friend. But let no one suppose that this king was singular in his wickedness. He is only a sample of what the heart of man is capable, and not the worst sample either.

When Elisha's Lord came in flesh and dwelt among men full of grace and truth, the great test came to men. What a Friend was Jesus to them! He went about doing good, healing the sick, blessing the children, cleansing the lepers, feeding the hungry, and weeping over them, so greatly did He love them. But they cried, "Away with Him! Crucify Him!" and leading Him out of their city to Golgotha, they murdered Him there. It was not the ignorant and degraded rabble that did it, but "the princes of the world crucified the Lord of Glory" (1 Corinthians 2:8). It was then and there that the sin of man rose up to Heaven, challenging the very supremacy of God, and crying for an answer of surrender to them on His part, or swift and exterminating judgment. But what was God's answer? Let us see what His answer to the wickedness of Jehoram by the mouth of Elisha was.

"Hear ye the Word of the Lord: Thus saith the Lord, To-morrow about this time shall a measure of fine flour be sold for a shekel, and two measures of barley for a shekel, in the gate of Samaria." It was an answer of grace through the very man whom the king would have destroyed; it was God's intervention on behalf of the afflicted people who had come to their wits' end. And here is illustrated God's answer to the challenge of man's sin at the Cross of Jesus. A feeble illustration, I admit, but there it is, like beams of grace shining in the twilight.

The Cross will be for ever the awful monument of the wickedness of men, yet it was also the great revelation of the love of God. God answered man's challenge, and declared His supremacy, but it was the supremacy of love, and where sin abounded grace did much more abound.

> *"The very spear that pierced His side*
> *Drew forth the Blood to save."*

"Thus it is written, and thus it behoved Christ to suffer, and to rise again from the dead the third day. And that repentance and remission of sins should be preached in His Name among all nations, BEGINNING AT JERUSALEM" (Luke 24:46, 47).

> *"O who would not boast in such love,*
> *And count all man's glory but dross."*

It seemed impossible that the word of Elisha could be fulfilled, and the lord on whose hand the king leaned, as godless a man as his master, scoffed at the prophet's words. He did not believe them. "Behold, if the Lord should make windows in Heaven, might this thing be?" he asked. Can God pour wheat and barley from Heaven? So he poured the scorning of an infidel upon the Word of the Lord, and showed that he knew nothing of the grace of God's heart, the power of His hand, and the infallibility of His Word.

This Samaria, foe-beleaguered and famine-stricken, is a vivid picture of sinful men in this world, of all, in fact, who have not been saved by grace. I have met people who have been startled by that statement, and who have asked: "What do you mean?" My answer has been, "You are besieged by a great army of enemies, who are seeking the destruction of your soul." And this is true of you, my unsaved reader. Do you say that you were not aware that you had a single enemy in the world? Well, you must have forgotten your sins, for your sins are your enemies! And death and the Devil, these are foes in whose eyes there is no pity, and who can show no mercy. And beyond all these there is the righteous judgment of God (Romans 2:5), for He will judge the secrets of men by Jesus Christ (Romans 2:16), and will render unto every man according to his deeds (Romans 2:6), and there is no respect of persons with God (Romans 2:11).

There are many, and I am one of them, who are full of gratitude to God that we discovered that we were beset with many enemies. And we had none more terrible than our SINS!

At the gate of the city were four leprous men, their dire condition had sharpened their wits and brought them to their senses and to a wise decision. "Why sit we here until we die?" they ask. We must do something. Shall we go into the city? No, that won't relieve us, for the famine is in the city, and we shall die there also. There is only one hope, and that is that our foes may be merciful, but if not, well, we had better face the situation courageously and at once, and leave the issue to God. It was on those lines that I reasoned when I awoke to my need, and it is after this manner that I invite my readers who do not yet know the saving grace of God to reason. You must do something, for you cannot save your own soul, nor can you satisfy your own heart's hunger, and the world cannot save and bless you; if you go to the world for salvation and satisfaction, you will find neither. The world passeth away and the lust thereof.

> *"Its grand fete days,*
> *And fashions and ways,*
> *Are all but perishing things."*

One of its most brilliant and enthusiastic votaries laid bare his empty heart when he wrote:

> *"Where is the world?...*
> *I looked for it—'tis gone!*
> *A globe of glass,*
> *Cracked, shivered, vanished,*
> *Scarce gazed upon ere a silent power*
> *Dissolved the glittering mass."*

And how weary of it all he must have been when he wailed:

> *"I fly like a bird of the air,*
> *In search of a home and a rest;*
> *A balm for the sickness of care,*
> *A bliss for a bosom unblest."*

There is no hope in the world for sinners; its pleasures cannot satisfy the hungry heart, its religion cannot save the guilty soul.

The one way of blessing is to face the grave questions of sin and death, of Satan's power, and of judgment to come, to be honest with yourself, and with God, to own the truth of your lost condition, and your need of a Deliverer. It is thus I interpret the story for you, and to take this way will issue in a great blessing, as the way of the leprous men did for them. They arose in the twilight and came to the camp of the Syrians, and did not find a single enemy there, "for the Lord had made the host of the Syrians to hear the noise of chariots and the noise of horses, even the noise of a great host. ... Wherefore they arose and fled in the twilight, and left their tents and their horses and their asses, even the camp as it was, and fled for their life."

It was a great deliverance, but only a feeble picture of one that is infinitely greater. The foes of the one who believes have not been scared from the field to which they might return when the scare was past, they have been confronted by the sinner's Champion and Substitute, and they have been put to utter rout. It was at Calvary that this great fight was fought and this great victory gained, and Jesus was the One Who stood there for us.

> *"Alone He bare the Cross,*
>   *Alone its grief sustained;*
> *His was the shame and loss,*
>   *And He the victory gained.*
> *The mighty work was all His own,*
> *Though we shall share His glorious Throne."*

And when these lepers came to the uttermost part of the camp, they went into one tent, and did eat and drink, and carried thence silver and gold and raiment, and went and hid it. Where they expected foes they found the feast, and were greatly enriched. And this is the experience of all who come to God through Christ. They come full of fear, believing that God is against them, a hard master, reaping where He had never sown, and instead they find that God is for them and against their enemies, that He has Himself secured salvation for them from the foes that threatened their souls, and has spread a feast for their starving souls. So the prodigal found it to be when he returned to his father, and so every soul finds it to be that turns to God.

These men were not content with what they found in the first tent, they went from tent to tent, enriching themselves as they went. In this they were a fine example for Christians of this day. How often do these rest content with their first knowledge of God and His blessing. The forgiveness of sins and the assurance of Heaven seem to be all that they desire to know, when there are the unsearchable riches of Christ for their enjoyment. We must go from tent to tent; we must grow in grace and in the knowledge of our Lord Jesus Christ, or we shall not know the extent of our wealth in Him. We must not neglect His grace. How beautifully it is put in that well-known verse, "For ye know the grace of our Lord Jesus Christ, that, though He was rich, yet for your sakes He became poor, that ye through His poverty might be rich" (2 Corinthians 8:9). But if we are to know this grace that has enriched us in its true blessedness, we must go in for it, we must go from tent to tent.

Then said these men one to another: "THIS IS A DAY OF GOOD TIDINGS, and we do not well to hold our peace. ... Come, therefore, now, that we may go and tell the king's household." It would have been a selfish and inhuman thing to have kept those good tidings to themselves. The blessing that they had found was for all the famished citizens of Samaria, and they were rightly moved when they said, "COME, THAT WE MAY GO AND TELL." These were good and evangelical words and should be in the hearts and mouths of all believing souls.

> *"Go and tell to all the world around,*
> *What a dear Saviour we have found."*

So they came to the city, and told the porters at the gate of it, and they, convinced by the enthusiasm of the men and the treasures they showed, which witnessed to the truth of their words, aroused His Majesty from his sleep.

First he made a confession: "They know that we be hungry." And that confession, if not on the lips is in the hearts of the multitudes that throng the world's pleasure haunts: "WE BE HUNGRY." It is written on their faces, it is heard in their hollow laughter, it shows itself in the frenzied rush for pleasure. Their appetites were never so considered as now, and never catered for with such abundance for the gratification of every lust and sense, and they were never so hungry.

Then the king jumped to a conclusion: "They have gone out of the camp to hide themselves in the field", said he; "and when we come out of the city they will catch us alive and get into the city." Which meant: "It's too good to be true." But one of his servants was a wise man, and proposed that at least they might send and see. "Let some take, I pray thee, five of the horses that remain in the city, and let us send and see." No one could question the wisdom of the proposal, and I would take it up and press it upon those who have doubts in their minds as to the blessedness of knowing the Lord. I would take up David's words and say, "O taste and see that the LORD is good; blessed is the man that trusteth in Him" (Psalm 34:8). "The proof of the pudding is in the eating." And those who have tasted say with united voice, "The Lord is gracious."

The advice was good, and they took therefore two chariot horses, and the king sent after the host of the Syrians, saying, "Go and see. AND THEY WENT AFTER THEM UNTO JORDAN, and lo, all the way was full of garments and vessels, which the Syrians had cast away in their haste. And the messengers returned and told the king."

The people went out and spoiled the tents of the Syrians. God fulfilled His own promise of deliverance and plenty, and all the famished inhabitants of the city rejoiced that day, but one man, and that man was the unbeliever. "Thou shalt see it with thine eyes," the prophet had said to him, "but thou shalt not taste thereof." And so it fell out unto him; for the people trod upon him in the gate, AND HE DIED. Twice over in the story do these words occur, as though to emphasise the doom of the unbeliever, and they bring to the mind those words that came from the lips of the Lord Himself: "He that believeth not shall be damned."

The rich man lifted up his eyes and saw Lazarus in the place of blessing; he saw it with his eyes, but he could not share in that blessing, for between him and it there was a great and impassable gulf fixed. They are unpopular words, but there they stand in God's Word, in which warnings are mingled with entreaties, and are all a proof of God's desire for the blessing of men.

"They went after them unto Jordan"

HOW THOSE WHO BELIEVE ARE RELIEVED BY THE TRUE MEANING OF THE CROSS OF CHRIST

"They took therefore two chariot horses, and the king sent after the host of the Syrians, saying, Go and see. And they went after them unto Jordan; and lo, all the way was full of garments and vessels which the Syrians had cast away in their haste. And the messengers returned and told the king."

2 KINGS 7:14, 15

Chapter 18
"They went after them unto Jordan"

What a relief it must have been to those starving Samaritans to find that Jordan was the end of their strong and remorseless foes. Traces of them there were every step of the way to that famous river, for the whole way was full of garments and vessels which the Syrians had cast away in their haste; but them they found not. With what eager steps would those messengers return to tell the king! What good news their report would be to the multitudes in the city. And, set free from fear of those terrible Syrians, with what relish they would turn to the feast so suddenly and so unexpectedly given them, according to the word of the man of God. And the silver and gold and raiment; the horses and the asses! It requires no vivid imagination to picture how quickly these would be appropriated by those astonished and triumphant Israelites.

Such is the end of the story so strikingly told, and so well worthy of being read, in 2 Kings 7. Story of deep interest, yet of important instruction, telling in pictorial language of "the better things" which the Gospel of God proclaims to us.

The Jordan typifies the death of Christ. Have we traced our foes to it and found it to be the death of them all? Every believer in that precious Saviour may do so, and rejoice in a complete and everlasting deliverance.

We had no foes more terrible than our SINS. How the guilt of them oppressed us! What a burden it was upon our consciences and souls as we staggered beneath the load of it to destruction! And the sins themselves—some of them went before us to judgment, proclaiming in trumpet tones as they went that rebels against God were coming that way, and others followed after, stealthy and sure, like a pack of sleuth hounds upon the trail of a fugitive, or an unerring detective on the track of the criminal, and ready to witness against us in the great Judgment Day! But whether they went before or after, the thought of them made us shudder with fear, for we were sure that our sins would find us out. Before, behind, and on every side of us they gathered like a strong host besieging a doomed city.

What a relief it was to us when we heard the Gospel—when we heard how the Son of God, whose precious Name is JESUS, had come to save us from our sins, and when, by faith, we saw Him bearing His Cross to Calvary as the Lamb of God Who beareth away the sin of the world! How great was the load that was laid upon Him there, for the Scripture saith, "The Lord hath laid on Him the iniquity of us all" (Isaiah 53:6), and "Who Himself bare our sins in His own body on the tree" (1 Peter 2:24). Because of our sins He suffered; "He was wounded for our transgressions, He was bruised for our iniquities: the chastisement of our peace was upon Him, and with His stripes we are healed" (Isaiah 53:5). As the scapegoat in Israel's history carried away, in figure, the sins of that nation into a land where no man dwelt, so in His death, when the waves of judgment rolled over Him, did our Scapegoat carry away our sins. They are cast into the depths of the sea (Micah 7:19); they are to be remembered no more (Hebrews 10:17); He was delivered for our offences that we might be justified from them all (Romans 4:25; Acts 13:39). How blessed for us to see Him, the Omnipotent Redeemer, going down into the dark waters of judgment with all our sins upon Him; to trace our sins to that sacred spot, and to see the mighty flood roll over them and HIM. Then on the third day, to see Him rise up without them, having made expiation for them, and be able to say to us, "Peace be unto you", and to know that now there is no condemnation for any who are in Him. In the death of Christ our sins were overwhelmed, and we are free.

And DEATH also, and him that had the power of it, what merciless foes were these! No kindness throbs in the bosom of the King of Terrors, no pity in the heart of the Devil; this we knew well, and how the thought of it made us dread the future—the last unavailing struggle, the silent grave and that which lies beyond! But the Gospel has brought a wonderful peace to our souls, for it has told us the tidings of Him Who partook of flesh and blood that, through death, He might destroy him that had the power of death, that is the Devil; and deliver them who through fear of death were all their lifetime subject to bondage (Hebrews 2:14, 15). As David laid the giant in the dust of Pas-dammin, and delivered Israel from the dread of him, so has our Lord delivered us; He has taken the sting out of death, and robbed the grave of its victory. We can trace our foes to His death, and find in that death the end of them all.

There were other foes also—our own evil selves—the flesh; the world with its allurements and snares; sin as a master, and many others; but the death of Christ is the way of deliverance from them all, whatsoever they be. And being set free, we may now feast upon the provision of God's grace for us, for where sin abounded grace does much more abound, and the gold, silver, and raiment, the wheat and the barley, all have their counterpart in blessed spiritual realities in Christianity. These are "the exceeding riches of God's grace" (Ephesians 2:7), "the unsearchable riches of Christ" (Ephesians 3:8), "the love of Christ which passeth knowledge", and "all the fulness of God" (Ephesians 3:19).

Yes, when we come to Christ the famine is turned into a feast, and where we expected foes and feared to meet them, there we find a full deliverance and God's plenteous provision for our need, and exceedingly abundantly more than we are able to ask or think.

Judgment without Mercy

HOW GRACE REFUSED MEANS
CERTAIN JUDGMENT

"And he went up from thence unto Bethel: and as he was going up by the way, there came forth little children out of the city, and mocked him, and said unto him, Go up, thou baldhead; go up, thou bald-head. And he turned back and looked on them, and cursed them in the Name of the LORD. And there came forth two she-bears out of the wood, and tare forty and two children of them. And he went from thence to Mount Carmel, and from thence he returned to Samaria."

2 KINGS 2:23-25

"But Gehazi, the servant of Elisha the man of God, said, Behold, my master hath spared Naaman this Syrian, in not receiving at his hands that which he brought: but, as the LORD liveth, I will run after him, and take somewhat of him. So Gehazi fol-lowed after Naaman. And when Naaman saw him running after him, he lighted down from the char-iot to meet him, and said, Is all well? And he said, All is well. My master hath sent me, saying, Behold, even now there be come to me from mount Ephraim two young men of the sons of the prophets: give them, I pray thee, a talent of silver, and two changes of garments."

2 KINGS 5:20-22

"And that lord answered the man of God, and said, Now, behold, if the LORD should make windows in heaven, might such a thing be? And he said, Behold, thou shalt see it with thine eyes, but shalt not eat thereof. And so it fell out unto him: for the people trode upon him in the gate, and he died."

2 KINGS 7:19, 20

Chapter 19
Judgment without Mercy

There are three cases of summary judgment in the ministry of Elisha. On first reading these we are surprised and perhaps a little shocked to find curses intermingled with blessings, and swift retribution running with longsuffering and compassion. But a careful consideration of them will convince us that they were just and right, and solemn warnings to us.

The first of these incidents occurred at the very beginning of the ministry of grace, and immediately after the healing of the waters at Jericho. The people ought to have been impressed by that miracle, but at Bethel they were not. Bethel had great traditions. Its meaning is "the house of God", and it was there that Jacob first met God. Above all places in the land the man of God ought to have had a welcome there, but instead the very children mocked him, and children by their public conduct show what their home training has been. I have no doubt that these children had heard their parents mock the prophet in private, they had grown up under an evil and godless influence. They were not "little children" in our meaning of the word, but youths and maidens, probably youths only, for the same word is used in chapter 4: "when the *child* was grown", and on several occasions in the Old Testament it is translated "young men". These children had reached the age of responsibility, and were accountable for their own actions. They made their choice, and rejected the man of grace. The judgment that came upon them was not only a judgment on their parents and the profane society in which they had been reared, but upon themselves also.

Their mocking words were not mere youthful rudeness. "Go up, thou baldhead. Go up, thou baldhead", meant more than that. It was their deliberate rejection of God's representative. It meant, "We do not want God in any way. Elijah has gone up, at least so it is reported, you go, too, and leave us in peace." The same spirit was shown by the men of the Lord's generation. "Wherewith shall I liken the men of this generation, and to what are they like?" He said, "They are like unto children sitting in the market place, and calling one to another and saying, We have piped unto you, and ye have not danced; we have mourned unto you, and ye have not wept. For John the Baptist came neither eating bread nor drinking wine, and ye say, He hath a devil. The Son of Man is come eating and drinking, and ye say, Behold, a gluttonous man and a wine-bibber, a friend of publicans and sinners" (Luke 7:31-34). Elijah and John came on the same ground; they pressed the claims of God upon the people, and exposed their sinful rebellion against Him, and had their ministry been heeded their hearers would have welcomed the grace that followed in Elisha, and above all in the Lord. But the people of Bethel hated the ministry of Elijah, they did not want to hear of God's rights or their rebellion, and they were glad when he took his departure for Heaven, and they wanted Elisha to go, too; they did not want to hear of the goodness of God; it was just as distasteful to them as His righteous claims. They did not want God in any way. What is there left for men if they cannot meet God's claims and won't have His grace? Nothing but judgment. This solemn fact is taught very early in man's history. To Cain God said, "If thou doest well, shalt thou not be accepted? And if thou doest not well, sin, or a sin-offering, lieth at the door." If Cain had been a righteous man, doing God's will and answering to all His holy and kindly claims, he would have been accepted on his own merits; but he was a sinner, and could claim nothing on that ground; but God had ordained a way by which sinful men could be justified and saved. He had provided the Sin-Offering, and in this His grace was displayed. It is all clearly taught in Romans 3:19-26. Cain rejected God's way of blessing for him, there was nothing left but God's judgment.

These youths were glad to be rid of Elijah, who pressed the claims; and they would not have Elisha, who brought the grace; and when grace is rejected judgment must act. It does not always act as swiftly as at Bethel, for God is longsuffering and very pitiful; but act it must, for what can God do with those who cannot meet His claims and will not have His pardoning grace in Christ? I know that eternal punishment is a most unpopular truth, but nothing else remains for those who reject God's salvation. God has done His best, His wisdom, power, and love are displayed in their Divine perfection in Jesus the Saviour, and there is no other salvation. Men cannot devise one, and God cannot provide another.

The second incident is that of Gehazi. He was a man of great knowledge and extraordinary privilege. He ought to have been a contented man, for he served the man of God, who could command God's resources in every time of need. But when the testing-time came, it found him out. All he seemed to care about was his own enrichment, and he schemed to turn the goodness of God to his own advantage. He was cursed with a covetous heart. He said, "Behold, my master hath spared Naaman the Syrian. ... As the LORD liveth I will run after him and take somewhat of him." He could not understand Elisha's desire that Naaman should not only know that there was a God in Israel, but that he should know the character of that God, that he should know that He freely gave that which was beyond all price. He did not rejoice in grace, he would have made Elisha and his God as grasping as himself.

How swift of foot his avarice made him that day, and Naaman, still wondering at the manner of the man of God, saw him running, and like the humbled and grateful man he was, he lighted down from his chariot to meet him. He met a liar and a covetous man, a man unchanged in heart in spite of all the grace of Elisha, a man who turned the grace of God into lasciviousness. He gave to him freely, and Gehazi became a richer man than his evil heart had hoped; but he spoilt the grace and clouded the revelation that the Syrian had received of God that day.

Poor wretch, he did not enjoy his ill-gotten gains for long. Elisha knew, his heart had gone with his unregenerated servant, sadly he had seen the whole transaction. "Is it a time to receive money, and to receive garments, and olive yards, and vineyards, and sheep, and oxen, and menservants, and maidservants?" Must we belie this grace of God that is so freely flowing out to needy men, and enrich ourselves by it, and reduce it to a commercial transaction? It is the sin of the Church in these last days, a sin in which it shamelessly boasts, "I am rich and increased in goods," it says, "and have need of nothing." "I know thy works," says the Lord, "I will spue thee out of My mouth" (Revelation 3:15-17). Terrible was the retribution. "The leprosy of Naaman shall cleave unto thee, and unto thy seed for ever. And he went out from his presence a leper as white as snow." Such was the judgment of God that fell upon the man who turned the grace of God into lasciviousness. We read of men of this type in the short Epistle of Jude: "For there are certain men crept in unawares, who were before ordained to this condemnation, ungodly men, turning the grace of God into lasciviousness, and denying the only Lord God and our Lord Jesus Christ" (verse 4).

The third incident is that of the lord on whose hand the king of Samaria leaned. He was a scoffer. When Elisha announced deliverance and plenty for the famine-stricken people of Samaria, he made a jest of it. This was his great sin, and it sprang up from the unbelief that was in his heart. "Behold," said he, "if the Lord should make windows in Heaven, might such a thing be." His words meant, "Elisha, we don't believe you." There are many incidents in these Old Testament records that show us that God cannot be trifled with, and that His Word must come true, but none more dramatic and striking than this: "Behold," said Elisha to him, "thou shalt see it with thine eyes, but thou shalt not eat thereof." And so it fell out unto him, for to him was given the charge of the gate when the great supplies were brought into the city from the Syrian camp, and the people trod on him in the gate, and he died, as the man of God had said. Twice is the fact recorded, and it closes the story. The three solemn words, "And he died", ring in our ears and remain in our thoughts when we have closed the Book. They are there for our admonition and as a solemn warning against unbelief. "He that believeth and is baptised shall be saved; He that believeth not *shall be damned*" (Mark 16:16), are words that answer to them in the New Testament. Words not spoken by an angel, or even by an apostle, but by the Lord Himself. They are wise people who hear His words and take heed to them.

Then we have these three cases of judgment recorded for our learning, teaching us that God is not mocked, that every man must give an account of himself to God, and that if grace is rejected nothing remains but judgment. May none of my readers reject the grace of God, or turn it into lasciviousness, or refuse to credit it, for those who do these things must share a common doom. "For this cause God shall send them strong delusion, that they should believe a lie; that they all might be damned who believed not the truth, but had pleasure in unrighteousness" (2 Thessalonians 2:11, 12).

The Weeping King and the Way of Victory

HOW VICTORY MAY FOLLOW DEFEAT

"And Jehoahaz besought the LORD, and the LORD hearkened unto him: for He saw the oppression of Israel, because the king of Syria oppressed them. And the LORD gave Israel a Saviour, so that they went out from under the hand of the Syrians; and the children of Israel dwelt in their tents as beforetime. ... Neither did he leave of the people to Jehoahaz, but fifty horsemen and ten chariots, and ten thousand footmen; for the king of Syria had destroyed them, and had made them like the dust by threshing. ... Now Elisha was fallen sick of his sickness whereof he died. And Joash, the king of Israel, came down unto him, and wept over his face, and said, O my father, my father, the chariot of Israel and the horsemen thereof. And Elisha said unto him, Take bow and arrows. And he took unto him bow and arrows. And he said to the king of Israel, Put thine hand upon the bow. And he put his hand upon it; and Elisha put his hands upon the king's hands. And he said, Open the window eastward. And he opened it. Then Elisha said, Shoot. And he shot. And he said, The arrow of the LORD's deliverance, and the arrow of deliverance from Syria: for thou shalt smite the Syrians in Apheck, till thou have consumed them. And he said, Take the arrows. And he took them. And he said unto the king of Israel, Smite upon the ground. And he smote thrice and stayed. And the man of God was wroth with him, and said, Thou shouldest have smitten five or six times; then hadst thou smitten Syria till thou hadst consumed it: whereas now thou shalt smite Syria but thrice."

2 KINGS 13:4, 5, 7, 14-19

Chapter 20
The Weeping King and the Way of Victory

The last incident in Elisha's life is not less instructive than the rest of his story. The chapter in which is it given shows the misery and poverty of the people in a few terse words: *"The king of Syria had oppressed them, and had destroyed them, and had made them like the dust of the threshing."* They were a backslidden people. They had turned their backs upon God, and gone their self-willed way after idols, and were but reaping what they had sown. Then King Jehoahaz besought the Lord, and we know that that was always the last resort of these children of Jacob; it had ever been a proof that they were at their wits' end. Yet the Lord hearkened to his cry, and this was evidence of the longsuffering of their God and ours. He is a God ready to forgive and plenteous in mercy. Hence we read: "He was gracious unto them, and had compassion on them, and gave them a Saviour, so that they went out from under the hand of the Syrians, and dwelt in their tents as aforetime", which means that they were free and safe and happy, as God always wished them to be.

But how reduced they were from the time when they followed the victorious Joshua into their God-given land, and what a change from the prosperous days of David and Solomon. It was their sins that had brought them so low, it was God's mercy that had preserved them from extinction.

There is surely an analogy between the decline of these children of Jacob and the Church on earth. We read of the days when "the churches had rest and were edified and walking in the fear of the Lord, and the comfort of the Holy Ghost were multiplied" (Acts 9:31); that "the disciples were filled with joy and the Holy Ghost" (Acts 13:52); and that "the Word of God grew and multiplied" (Acts 12:24). Those were great days, when with one heart and one mind Christians strove together for the Faith, and had "joy unspeakable and full of glory" (1 Peter 1:8); "rivers of living water" (John 7:38) flowed from them, and "from them sounded out the Word of the Lord, and in every place their faith God-ward was spread abroad" (1 Thessalonians 1:8). We are conscious that things are different now, that we have reached the days in which "evil men and seducers have waxed worse and worse, deceiving and being deceived" (2 Timothy 3:13), and that in Christendom and in the Name of Christ sound doctrine is not endured, but, having itching ears, men heap to themselves teachers of their own sort, who will preach fables to them, and not the truth. Not all are like this; there are some who are aggressively orthodox, but with no heart for Christ. They have a Name to live, but are dead. Others again have sincerely desired to walk in the truth. They have cast off all authority but the Word of God, and yet how they have blundered and failed, and those who are nearest to God will feel it the most. And for those who feel it, is there any remedy, any hope of recovery? Yes,

thank God there is, and this hope lies first in the longsuffering love and unfailing compassion of our God. He is
the Father of mercies and the God of all comfort, and as
He gave to impoverished Israel a Saviour, who without
doubt was Elisha, so will He still deliver His people.
Elisha's presence in the land seems to have been forgotten
for forty years, and yet he was there, ready to show the
kindness of God to the people whenever they turned to
Him. We know that he speaks to us of Christ, Who is our
great Deliverer right through to the end. In Christ there is
hope, for He dieth no more, as did Elisha; "He ever liveth
to make intercession for us" (Hebrews 7:25).

God never did and never will turn away from the cry of
His people, for He loves them with an unchanging love,
and while He must often chasten them because of their
waywardness, for "whom the Lord loveth He chasteneth,
and scourgeth every son that He receiveth" (Hebrews
12:6), yet He will not give them up. It was of these wilful
children of Jacob that He said: "I have loved thee with an
everlasting love, and with lovingkindness will I draw thee"
(Jeremiah 31:3), and again, "can a woman forget her suck-
ing child, that she should not have compassion on the son
of her womb? Yea, they may forget, yet will I not forget
thee. Behold, I have engraved thee upon the palms of my
hands" (Isaiah 49:15, 16). And if His love to Israel was so
great and faithful, and if they always proved it to be so
when they turned from their backsliding to Him, how
much more shall we prove it in these "more abundant"
days of Gospel grace. He has brought us into His family,
all who have believed in the Son of His love are His children, and they form His Church in which He is to have
glory in Christ Jesus unto all the generations of the age of
ages.

It is in the Epistle which unfolds for us the favour and joy of our relationship to God as our Father that we read: "If we confess our sins, He is faithful and just to forgive us our sins, and to cleanse us from all unrighteousness" (1 John 1:9). And wherever there has been backsliding this is the way of restoration, and restoration to communion with our God and Father and our Lord Jesus Christ means deliverance from oppression and defeat, and spiritual revival. We come out from under the hand of the Syrian, and dwell in our tents as aforetime. We enjoy our blessings and live as God's children should.

Now we come to God's last deliverance of Israel through Elisha. The prophet was dying, and the king hastened to his side. His tears indicated that his heart was sorely burdened, and his cry, "My father, my father, the chariot of Israel and the horsemen thereof", showed that he realised that without Elisha they would be an orphaned people, nor could they hope for any victories over their foes. If only that people had realised that continually what a different history theirs would have been! But here comes a challenge to every one of us. Do we realise how indispensable the Lord Jesus is to us? What should we do without Him? If He had ceased to be the Administrator of God's grace to us, where should we be? The very thought is an appalling one. Not for worlds would we be cut off from Him. Then let us appreciate Him with a greater fervour, and make use of Him with a larger faith. Let us consider Him in this twofold character. "Like as a father pitieth his children, so the LORD" (Psalm 103:13). He cares for us with a tender and constant care, and He is our protector from every enemy. These two sides of the truth have been illustrated by the wings of the mother bird. The soft down in which the young birds nestle tells of the tender care of our Lord, the strong quills that protect them from the enemy tell of the protection we have in Him against our foes. We may well take up the words of this weeping king, and say to our Lord with a greater and more spiritual intelligence, "My Father, my Father, the chariot of Israel and the horsemen thereof." And we can take up this cry without tears, except for our own foolish backsliding, and for this and the impoverished condition of the Church we might well weep; but we can take it up with joy, for our Saviour dieth no more. He has said, "I am He that liveth and was dead, and behold, I am alive for evermore" (Revelation 1:18); and again, "I will never leave thee nor forsake thee." So that we may boldly say, "The Lord is my Helper. I will not fear what men shall do unto me" (Hebrews 13:5, 6). And He is our Leader, the Captain of our salvation.

And now we learn in a new way the way of victory, when all human hope is dying. "Open the window eastward", said the prophet. Surely a word to us to keep our faces towards the sunrising. We must not be occupied with the failure or grow depressed in the dying dispensation. It may be true, and it is, that the day is far spent, but we look for the Saviour. Hope of the glory yet to come is a great tonic for the drooping spirit; it is salvation to those who have it. They can lift up their heads, for this hope is a helmet to them.

> *"Our hearts beat high,*
> *The dawn is nigh*
> *Which ends our pilgrim story*
> *In His appointed glory."*

This outlook is important, and in this closing chapter of our book we would give it emphasis. It is the outward and upward look that revives the soul. And the sure word of promise constrains us to this steadfast look. Light springs up anew for the soul that faces the sunrising. It is renewal of strength for those who wait upon the Lord.

Then upon the hands of the king the prophet placed his hands. Here there was the surrender of the king's strength. Elisha's hand was to guide that arrow in its flight. The king was a passive instrument, and yet so identified with Elisha's strength in his surrender to him, that the act of shooting was his. It is only thus that the bow of any servant of the Lord can abide in strength. It was so with Joseph. He was the target of his enemies, then "the arms of his hands were made strong by the hand of the mighty God of Jacob, and from thence is the Shepherd, the Stone of Israel" (Genesis 49:24). POWER, PRESERVATION, PERMANENCE. The might of God to direct us in our warfare, the Shepherd of Israel to preserve us in every danger, and the unmoveable Rock upon which we are sure-based—all are there for the one who abandons any strength that he has thought he possessed, and yielded himself wholly to God.

God is always greater than our faith. Our faith is feeble and limited. His supplies are boundless and inexhaustible. "Ye have not because ye ask not" (James 4:2), and often we dishonour God and miss much because we ask and expect so little. So Joash struck three times, and stayed when he might have struck five or six times. Indeed, he ought to have continued striking until Elisha told him to stop. "When will you cease asking favours of me?" asked a great monarch of a persistent courtier. "When your Majesty ceases to give", was the shrewd reply. "ASK, and ye shall receive, that your joy may be full", said the Lord. "For the Father Himself loveth you, because ye have loved Me, and have believed that I came out from God" (John 16:24, 27).

It is our desire to be more than conquerors through Him that loved us. This is the way, to have our hands yielded up to His, and to ask and to expect. To smite at His bidding, and to continue to smite, that "the world, the flesh, and the Devil" may indeed be smitten and defeated foes. If any man is to be an overcomer in his own life, and a helper and deliverer of others, this is the only way. The story of King Joash and the aged prophet was surely written that we might be admonished to this end.

"And Elisha Died ... and the Man Revived"

HOW LIFE SPRINGS OUT OF DEATH

"And Elisha died, and they buried him. And the bands of the Moabites invaded the land at the coming in of the year. And it came to pass, as they were burying a man, that, behold, they spied a band of men; and they cast the man into the sepulchre of Elisha: and when the man was let down, and touched the bones of Elisha, he revived and stood up on his feet."

2 KINGS 13:20, 21

Chapter 21
"And Elisha Died ... and the Man Revived"

THE death of Elisha was the snapping of the last link of Israel with God; after it they fell into complete apostasy, joined with an alien power to fight against their brethren of Judah, and were finally carried away into a captivity from which they have not been recovered unto this day. As a people these ten tribes, and indeed the whole race of Israel, are dead indeed, morally and spiritually dead. But here comes in an amazing thing. The corpse of a dead man cast into the sepulchre of Elisha, and coming into contact with his bones, sprang into life. The miracle is a great prophecy. It tells of the resurrection, restoration, and final blessing of that dead nation. "All Israel shall be saved" (Romans 11:26). This is a necessity for the glory of God and for our sakes also; for the integrity of God's Word depends upon it. He has spoken great things of Israel's future under the sway of great David's greater Son, and if His Word cannot be fulfilled, what guarantee have we that His Word to us will hold good? But not one jot or tittle of His Word can fail, and "the gifts and calling of God are without repentance", and this is most conclusively proved in Romans 9, 10, 11. Ezekiel's vision of the valley of dry bones (chapter 37), is to have a wonderful fulfilment, and "many that sleep in the dust shall awake, some to everlasting life, and some to shame and everlasting contempt" (Daniel 12:2).

But by what means and upon what righteous basis will God bring this about? God has only one basis upon which He can bless them, and bring them out of death into life, and that is the basis upon which all are blest who are blest at all—THE DEATH OF CHRIST. Upon this basis He can be a just God and a Saviour. In that death His righteousness was manifest, and the effect of that righteousness is peace for all who believe now, as it will be peace for Israel when they are raised up out of the moral and spiritual death in which they lie.

We delight in Isaiah 53. What a wonderful chapter it is. Much joy and blessing have we drawn from it, for Christ and His suffering love and His great sacrifice for sin are its theme. Yet in the first place it belongs to Israel. In the day when through sore tribulation they shall be brought to deep repentance, they will say, "He was wounded for our transgressions, He was bruised for our iniquities; the chastisement of our peace was upon Him, and with His stripes we are healed." They will realise that He was cut off out of the land of the living for their transgressions, and that when He poured out His soul unto death, they were the transgressors for which He made His prayer. And they will see Him Whom they pierced, and will say, "What are these wounds in Thine hands?" And then shall they mourn for Him, as one mourneth for his only son, and as one that is in bitterness for his firstborn (Zechariah 12, 13). They will realise that only through His death could they have life. They will come thus into vital contact with His death, and just as Thomas, the unbeliever, cried out when he beheld the wounded body of his Lord, "My Lord and my God", so will they say when they see the Lord, "Lo, this is our God; we have waited for Him, and He will save us; this is the LORD; we have waited for Him, we will be glad and rejoice in His salvation" (Isaiah 25:9). It will be true then: "Thy dead men shall live together, with my dead body shall they arise. Awake and sing, ye that dwell in the dust" (Isaiah 26:19). But all this blessing will come to them because their Messiah suffered for them. His soul was made an offering for sin on their behalf. He died for them. Even the godless Sadducee, Caiaphas, was compelled to speak of this when he and his confreres in wickedness plotted the murder of Jesus. "Ye know nothing at all," said he, "nor consider that it is expedient for us, that one man should die for the people, and that the whole nation perish not. And this spake he not of himself; but being high priest that year, he prophesied that Jesus should die for the nation: and not for that nation only, but that He should gather together in one the children of God that were scattered abroad" (John 11:49-52).

Every lover of the Lord Jesus will rejoice to know that He is yet to see of the travail of His soul and be satisfied in regard to Israel. Yes, this people who thrust Him from them, when He came full of grace and truth to them, and cried, "Away with Him! Crucify Him!" and joined hands with the pagan Romans in His murder, and by their own act apostatised from God and forfeited all claim upon Him, are yet to learn that God hath raised up Him Whom they took and by wicked hands crucified and slew, and that through Him and His very death that they brought about they may be pardoned and blest, and restored to favour in their own promised land.

He has said: "I will heal their backsliding, I will love them freely" (Hosea 14:4). And no more will the Lord have to weep over them as He did when He looked on their city, and said: "O Jerusalem, Jerusalem, thou that killest the prophets and stonest them that are sent unto thee, how often would I have gathered thy children together, even as a hen gathereth her chickens beneath her wings, and ye would not" (Matthew 23:37); but to them it shall be said, "The Lord thy God in the midst of thee is mighty; He will save; He will rejoice over thee with joy; He will rest in His love, He will joy over thee with singing" (Zephaniah 3:17).

As it will be with Israel in that coming day of Millennial glory, so it is now. There is no life for any sinner except through the death of our Lord Jesus Christ. Christ crucified is a stumbling-block to the Jew, and to the Greek foolishness; but to those who are saved He is the power of God and the wisdom of God, and God's love is commended to us in Him. Happy are all those who can say, "I am crucified with Christ; nevertheless, I live, yet not I, but Christ liveth in me" (Galatians 2:20). And "the love of Christ constraineth us, because we thus judge, that if one died for all, then were they all dead; and that He died for all, that they which live should not henceforth live unto themselves, but unto Him which died for them and rose again" (2 Corinthians 5:14, 15).

*   *   *   *   *

Elisha is introduced to us first as a servant with a heart of love in his breast, and a great readiness to obey, and a care for those about him. For when Elijah called him, he was serving with a team of oxen, and in becoming servant to Elijah he did not forget his father and mother, or the needs of his poor neighbours, for he slew his oxen and boiled their flesh, and gave unto the people, and they did eat. Then he arose and followed Elijah, and ministered unto him (1 Kings 19:19-21). And by this first incident in his life we are reminded of the words of our Lord: "The Son of Man came not to be ministered unto, but to minister" (Mark 10:45). He was the servant of His Father's will, and the Servant of man's need, and then He added, "To give His life a ransom for many." "Being found in fashion as a man, He humbled Himself and became obedient unto death, even the death of the cross. Wherefore God hath highly exalted Him, and given Him a Name that is above every name: that at the Name of Jesus every knee should bow, of things in heaven, and things in earth, and things under the earth; and that every tongue should confess that Jesus Christ is Lord, to the glory of God the Father" (Philippians 2:8-11). And a multitude that no man can number will owe the eternal life that they will enjoy to His death, and will adore Him for ever as the Lamb that was slain.

DELIVERING GRACE